CONTENTS

KT-115-943

INTRODUCTION

Clothes are useful; they can keep us warm or cool, cheer us up with bright colours and pamper us with soft textures. They also serve as signs of our identity. They send out messages about us, describing our place in the world.

The skirt worn by this Masai woman from East Africa shows that she is married and belongs to a wealthy family.

Belonging

Clothes can show which tribe or nation we belong to. They may also reveal our gender, and whether we are married or single. Clothes can make a political statement, or proclaim our religion. They can give onlookers clues about the work we do, how much money we have, and the image we hope to create for ourselves.

Barefoot history

The early ancestors of modern humans left footprints behind at Olduvai Gorge in Tanzania, Africa. This illustration is based on fossil finds.

Shoes, boots, socks and sandals are all recent inventions. For millions of years, men, women and children walked barefoot, like animals, and the soles of their feet hardened to cope. Later migration to colder climates necessitated the wearing of shoes.

FASHION
A HISTORY

Copyright © ticktock Entertainment Ltd 2009
First published in Great Britain by ticktock Media Ltd,
The Old Sawmill, 103 Goods Station Road, Tunbridge Wells, Kent TN1 2DP

ticktock project editor: Vicky Garrard
project designer: Trudi Webb

ISBN-13: 978-1-84898-008-2 pbk

Printed in China

Picture credits (t=top; b=bottom; c=centre; l=left; r=right)

Alamy: 42l. Jason Alden/Rex Features: 88t. Ancient Art and Architecture: 30t, 30b. Bridgeman Art Library: 29b. Tiago Chediak/Wikimedia Commons: 85. Condé Nast Archive/Corbis: OFCcr. Corbis: 9b 38l, 38-39, 40l, 41t, 43c, 46-47, 70r, 71b, 75b, 77t, 78b, 80b, 81b. Marion Curtis/Rex Features: 91t. iStock: OFCc, OFCb. Jon Feinstein/ Wikimedia Commons: 93b. Fine Art Photographic Library/Corbis: 63t. Fort Rock Museum: 10b. Getty Images for IMG: 84t. Alessia Pierdomenico/Reuters/Corbis: 84b. Rex Features: 5t, 62b. Christian Schmidt/zefa/Corbis: 91b. Shutterstock: OFCtr, OFCct, 24b, 81t, 89, 92t, 92b, 93t, OBC (all). Charles Sykes/Rex Features: 90. Werner Forman Archive: 6r, 11b, 12l, 12-13, 13t, 13b, 14t, 14b, 15t, 15b, 16l, 16-17, 17t, 17b, 18t, 18b, 18-19, 18t, 19b, 20l, 20-21, 21l, 21r, 22t, 22b, 23l, 23r, 24-25, 25t, 25b, 26t, 26b, 27t, 27b, 29t, 31t, 31b, 39t, 50-51, 51t, 51b, 54-55c. WireImage/Getty Images: 86b, 86-87t.

Every effort has been made to trace copyright holders, and we apologise in advance for any omissions. We would be pleased to insert the appropriate acknowledgments in any subsequent edition of this publication.

Trend-setters

Fashion is about popular styles of clothing – it can be strange, exciting or experimental. Twice a year top fashion designers show their latest styles to journalists. Few of these clothes are ever worn by people outside the fashion or entertainment industries. Instead, they are designed to highlight new trends – such as short skirts or wide shoulders – that will be copied by manufacturers making mass-market clothes to sell.

Clothes for everyday

In the past, most ordinary people could only afford one set of clothes at a time. They wore them everyday. Compared with elaborate fashions, worn only by rich people, everyday clothes were practical and long lasting. Their designs changed very slowly. Most were worn - and mended - year after year, until they finally fell to pieces.

Did you know...?

'Haute Couture' is the French phrase for 'high fashion' — it's pronounced 'Oat Coot-yoor'.

New fashions are displayed by supermodels, accompanied by the latest music.

Members of the same age group often choose similar clothes.

THE FIRST EVERYDAY CLOTHES

No-one knows exactly when the first clothes were made. But many historians think clothing was invented some time between 100,000 BC – 50,000 BC. This was the time when modern humans (homo sapiens) left their warm homeland in Africa and migrated to live in colder parts of the world.

Furs and hides

The first clothes were made from the furs or hides (animal skins) of large wild animals. They were preserved by rubbing with fat or hanging over a cool, smoky fire. After around 30,000 BC, most clothes-makers used stone knives to trim skins and needles of bone or mammoth-ivory to sew them together.

Skins and things

Sioux Chief's war leggings dating from the end of the 18th century.

The first sewn garments were sleeveless tunics, worn by men or women. They were made from two cut and shaped animal skins, stitched together at the shoulders. Wearers either went bare legged, or wrapped their feet and legs with strips of animal skin. Similar methods were still used by native peoples in North America in the 18th century.

Most people wore a combination of Furs and skins in 50,000 BC .

Squeezing and weaving

Early people also created clothes by processing natural fibres. They twisted tall plant stems into string, and hammered tree-bark to make fabric. They produced felt by boiling and squeezing animal hair, and spun thread by twirling plant fibres or sheep's wool. At first, string and thread were only used for nets, bags and braids. But later thread was woven into cloth, on wooden frames called looms.

The earliest woven garments were sheep's wool blankets. They looked similar to the traditional blankets worn by Masai men in Africa today.

Did you know...?

Prehistoric people used to sew skins and furs together with animal sinews (bands of stretchy flesh that attach muscles to bones) or lengths of hair from animals' manes and tails.

Silk and cotton

Around 3000 BC, people living in India and China found ways of creating finer, more delicate fibres. Chinese workers unwound miles of natural silk thread from cocoons made by silk-moth grubs, and wove it into shimmering gauze (thin, transparent fabric). At the same time, Indus Valley farmers harvested fluffy cotton wool (the fibre around cotton-seeds), spun it into thread then wove it into light, cool cloth.

Indian saris – long lengths of fabric, carefully folded at the waist and draped round the body – were some of the earliest clothes to be made from cotton cloth, and later in silk (right).

THE FIRST FASHIONS AND FINERY

Everywhere, in all past ages, men and women have worn jewellery. They have also painted themselves and each other with dramatic designs. Almost certainly, early people wore jewellery and make-up long before they started to wear clothes.

Not like others

A Congolese tribal dancer wearing a traditional costume and mask.

For many centuries, ceremonial clothes sent out a message that the person wearing them was special. They might have been a priest or a shaman (someone who practices sorcery for healing). Their clothes had magic or symbolic meanings, designed to show purity or spiritual power.

Slow to change

Early clothes were often very slow to change. Historians have suggested two reasons for this. Firstly, before machines and fast methods of transport were invented, clothes could only be made by hand, from local materials. The second is social organisation. In traditional cultures, there were often few opportunities for ordinary people to change their occupation, status or peer-group. The clothes they were allowed to wear were decided by their place in society, and strictly limited by custom or law.

This South African shaman is wearing special clothes to show his importance within his tribe.

Status symbols

Early clothes and body ornaments were like modern fashions in some important ways. To show leaders' wealth and status, they were made of valuable materials, such as furs, feathers, amber, ivory, gold and precious stones. The most costly of these status symbols were exotic – that is, they could not be found locally but had to be imported from a long way away. As early as around 10,000 BC, traders travelled vast distances to meet merchants from distant lands at fairs (trading camps), and barter (swap) valuable finery. Walking there and back home might take many months of each year.

Valuable amber beads like these were traded over long distances in the Middle East.

Did you know...?

The word 'jewel' comes from an Ancient Roman word meaning 'plaything'.

Decorated all over

Early people used jewellery and make-up to decorate many parts of their bodies. They made headdresses, necklaces, arm-bands, ear-rings, nose-rings, breast-plates and lip-plugs (plates inserted under the lower lip). They tied decorations around their toes, thighs and ankles, and made pretty pins from wood or bone to fasten their clothes together.

This man from Papua New Guinea is wearing a headdress and jewellery made from feathers, seeds, plant fibres and shells.

Footwear was not invented until late in human history. The first shoes or boots were probably made between 50,000 BC – 20,000 BC. The oldest known image of people wearing foot-coverings comes from a rock-painting in Spain, made around 15,000 years ago.

The first footwear was made of the same materials as other early clothing: animal skins and plant fibres. Strips of hide or fur were wrapped around the feet and lower legs and held in place by rawhide laces. In cold climates, they kept wearers warm. Plant fibres, such as bark and dried grass, were twisted together to make simple sandals. These protected feet from thorns, stones, biting insects and burning sand in hot climates.

Skins and fibres

Traditional sandals made from plant fibres by Aboriginal people in Australia still follow very ancient designs.

Woven soles

By around 10,000 BC, footwear design had become more sophisticated. Soles for sandals were woven to fit the precise shape of the foot, and were fastened over the instep and around the ankle by neat strings of twisted plant fibre.

The oldest surviving footwear so far discovered was a pair of pre-contact sandals found at Fort Rock, Oregon, USA, dating from between 10,500 BC -9300 BC.

First hats

Birds with fine feather crests display them
to attract a mate. Fierce male lions have
magnificent manes of hair. Early humans
admired these symbols, and copied
them. They made headdresses for
powerful people. They hoped these
would give their leaders a share
in the wild creatures' power.

Archaeologists do not yet know
when the first hats were made.
But it is likely that early humans,
over 2 million years ago, may have
draped animal skins over their heads
for warmth in cold conditions, or shaded their
faces from the Sun with mats of leaves or grass.

This tribal leader from the Ecuadorian rainforest is wearing a colourful feather headdress, decorated with rainforest flowers.

Fur hats

By 100,000 years ago, men
and women had learnt to
make tools that could cut
furs and animal hide and
stitch them together.
They made simple
tunics and trousers
and, archaeologists
believe, hats as well.

Warm fur hoods, like this one worn by an Inuit from Alaska, may first have been made 100,000 years ago.

11

ANCIENT EGYPT AND ITS NEIGHBOURS

The climate of Egypt in North Africa is hot and very dry. Because of this, the Ancient Egyptians wore very few clothes. However, they were some of the earliest men and women to wear clothing made from woven fabric, rather than animal skins and furs.

Simple shapes

Wall Painting of Ramses III wearing an elaborate loincloth.

Egyptian clothes were simple – just lengths of fabric, folded into convenient shapes then pinned or tied around the body. For working in their fields, Egyptian men wore brief loincloths (strips of fabric wrapped between the legs like a nappy) or short lengths of fabric wound around the waist, like kilts (wrapped skirts). Both styles were held in place by knotting two ends of the garment together, or by belts made of leather or rope.

Unchanging styles

Women's clothes were made of a larger piece of cloth, wrapped right around the body from the breast to the ankle. Sometimes, two small pieces were used instead, and stitched together at the sides. Both methods created a long, narrow, tube-shaped garment, which was stopped from slipping down by two wide shoulder straps. It stayed in style for almost 2,000 years.

A straight, simple, narrow dress was everyday wear for most Egyptian women. Natural cream and white (for linen) and fawn or grey (for wool) were the usual shades.

Did you know...?
The favourite fabric of Egyptian Pharaohs (kings) was crisp, cool, white linen. The Egyptians believed the gods wore white linen in heaven.

Sleeves and pleats

After around 1530 BC, invaders from West Asia introduced new clothing designs. Egyptian men and women began to wear extra lengths of fabric draped loosely over their arms and shoulders. These created wide, baggy sleeves, and were held in place, front and back, by tight waist belts or metal pins.

Men also began to wear double-layer kilts with extra front and side panels. Pleated clothes draped gracefully, trapped cool air close to the body, and let the wearer move freely.

The Egyptian man on the left wears a kilt with a wide, pleated front panel. The man on the right wears a simpler, old-style kilt, tied at the waist.

Furs and fringes

At night, when desert temperatures fell quickly, Egyptian men and women wrapped themselves in warm blankets, woven from sheep's wool. But their neighbours in the colder, mountainous lands of West Asia continued to wear thick, bulky cloaks of sheepskin and fur. These Asians also wove woollen cloth decorated with fringes and tassels to look like shaggy animal skins.

This Sumerian stele from the lands east of Egypt depicts a man receiving the Law Code. The figure on the left wears a heavy cloak typical of the style of the time.

ANCIENT EGYPT AND ITS NEIGHBOURS

Ancient Egyptian civilisation lasted for 3,000 years. During that time, clothing styles hardly changed at all among ordinary people. But for the rich, a few new fashions were created, in clothes, wigs and jewels.

Pharaoh Tutankhamun (reigned 1336–1327 BC) is wearing a long pleated skirt.

Wonderful wigs

In Egypt, fashionable people and some top entertainers displayed their status and artistic flair by their choice of jewels and wigs. Even without clothes, these were still very expensive, and symbols of prestige. The earliest wigs were short and simple. But after around 1500 BC, long wigs became fashionable. Many were decorated with beads and ringlets (long, loose curls). After around 300 BC, natural hair replaced wigs.

Longer, fuller fashions

From around 3000 BC, men made short skirts and women created dresses by wrapping lengths of fabric around the body. By 2100 BC, men's and women's fashions became longer and looser. Around 1500 BC, important men and women wore long, pleated skirts or gowns, made of fine, transparent fabric held in place by belts around the waist. Lengths of cloth were also draped over the shoulders to create wide, airy sleeves.

Two musicians and a dancer have put on their best wigs to entertain nobles at a feast, from the Tomb of Nakht, c. 1567–1320 BC.

Classic colours

In Egypt, white was the most fashionable colour. Linen (made from flax) – the Egyptians' favourite fabric - was difficult to dye, but could be bleached by stretching it out to dry in Egypt's burning-hot midday sun. Among neighbouring peoples, deep purple was the most fashionable and expensive colour. It was made by rotting murex shellfish in sea-water for months or years. This messy, smelly process created a deep purple dye that bonded to wool, or to prestige Asian fabrics like imported cotton and silk.

Murex shellfish, used to make dye, were fished from the warm waters of the eastern Mediterranean Sea.

Fashions for burial

In regions like North Africa, and neighbouring West Asia, where clothes styles changed slowly, fine, fashionable jewellery was an important symbol of wealth and status. Some of the world's best metalworkers lived and worked in Sumer (now Iraq and Syria), around 2000 BC. They created fabulous new finery to be worn by the royal family – even when they were buried in splendid 'burial pit' tombs. These jewels included diadems and other hair ornaments, in local Sumerian style.

Did you know...?

In Ancient Egypt women rulers, and young boy pharaohs (kings) wore false beards for special occasions.

This jewellery was discovered in the tomb of Queen Pu-Abi of Ur (Sumer's capital city).

15

In many early societies, like Ancient Egypt, footwear was a sign of status. Only rich people could afford to purchase shoes or sandals and only royal or noble families were allowed to wear them all the time.

Going Barefoot

These Egyptian men are not wearing any shoes while baking bread. This was usual practise in ancient Egypt.

Most ordinary Egyptian men, and all Egyptian women, went barefoot both inside and outside. In the hot, dry climate of Egypt, their feet did not get wet or cold, but they did get cut, bruised, dusty and dirty. Egyptian medical texts contain many remedies for sore, aching feet.

A Pharaoh's footwear

The Ancient Egyptians buried their Pharaohs (kings) and nobles in magnificent tombs, with everything they would need in the afterlife, including carvings. Sandals were the most common footwear design. Most had a flat sole, toe-post and wide straps over the instep or round the heel. A Pharaoh's sandal might be made of gold.

This gold statue of Pharaoh Tutankhamun shows him wearing typical Ancient Egyptian sandals. Pharaohs' sandals were often decorated with real gold and precious stones.

An expert trade

Egyptian sandals were made by expert craft-workers. They used a wide variety of materials, including wood, burlap cloth, palm-fronds and plaited papyrus (reeds that grew beside the River Nile). They were also some of the first people to use tanned leather.

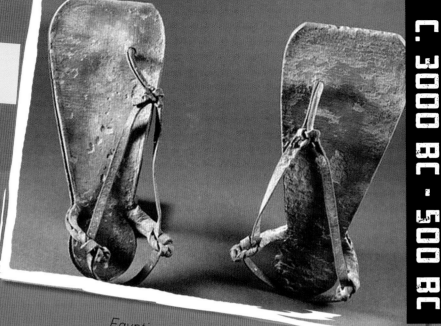

Egyptian tanned leather sandals, made around 3000 BC.

Did you know...?

In Ancient Egypt, slaughter-house workers often wore high-heeled shoes so that their feet would not touch the blood from animals they killed.

Climbing and riding

Neighbouring West Asian peoples had to survive in high mountains and cold weather. So they developed footwear that was suitable for climbing up steep, snowy paths, or for riding long distances. Hittite mountain villagers (who lived in Turkey around 2000 BC) made tough ankle boots with turned-up toes.

Clay model of a Hittite boot, made around 2000 BC.

ANCIENT EGYPT AND ITS NEIGHBOURS

For coolness and extra cleanliness, Egyptian men and women shaved their heads or cut their hair very short. Children had their heads shaved, too, except for a strand left trailing beside one ear. This was called 'the lock of youth'.

Cool and clean

These Egyptian builders would have had to wash in the River Nile – if they washed at all.

Ordinary people had to wash in the River Nile. Wealthy families had shower rooms, where their personal slaves poured water over them as they stood below.

Wigs

Rich men and women wore elaborate wigs made of human or animal hair for fashion, protection from the elements and to cover up baldness. Styles varied over the centuries, from long ringlets or thick shoulder-length braids to short, tight curls. On special occasions, wigs might be decorated with beads and scented with perfume. Ordinary people could not afford fancy wigs. They wore rough wigs of plant fibre, or simple lengths of cloth tied round their heads.

Left: A wig of curled and braided human hair, made around 1500 BC.

Different crowns

Ancient Egyptian art often shows pharaohs wearing different crowns, such as the khepresh (war crown) and pschent (double crown). The pschent was a symbol of the two regions of Egypt, united around 3100 BC. The top of the crown was white, representing Upper (southern) Egypt. The lower part was red, signifying Lower (northern) Egypt.

This tomb model shows King Tutankhamun wearing the 'war crown' of the pharaohs.

A bust thought to be of King Amenemhat IV. It shows the pharaoh wearing the nemes headcloth with a uraeus.

Did you know...?

A conical straw hat painted on a cave wall in the Egyptian city of Thebes is one of the earliest known depictions of a hat.

The sign of a king

Royal crowns and headdresses, called a nemes, were usually decorated with a fierce uraeus (rearing cobra). This was the symbol of the goddess Wadjet, a special protector of kings. In neighouring Nubia, rulers wore diadems on top of short hair. The diadem featured cobra symbols and two rearing cobra decorations were also placed over the king's forehead.

Statuette of a Nubian King (7th century BC) showing diadem.

19

THE ANCIENT GREEK WORLD

Greek traders travelled throughout the Mediterranean region, making contact with peoples in Europe, Africa and West Asia and picking up clothing fashions along the way. Greek clothes were made of Greek sheep's wool, Turkish linen, and silk imported from China.

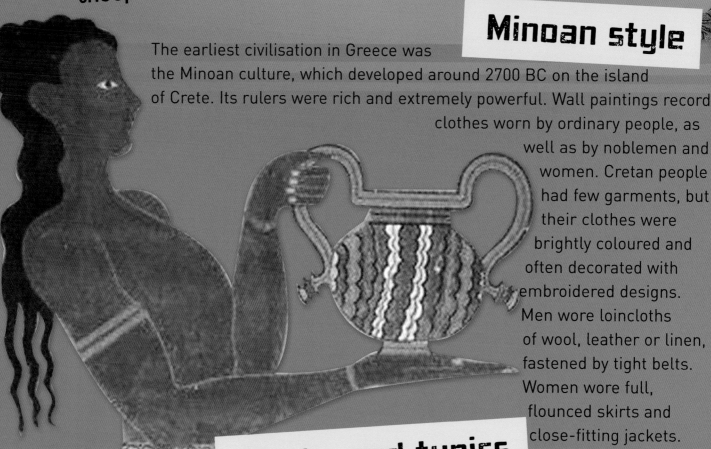

Minoan style

The earliest civilisation in Greece was the Minoan culture, which developed around 2700 BC on the island of Crete. Its rulers were rich and extremely powerful. Wall paintings record clothes worn by ordinary people, as well as by noblemen and women. Cretan people had few garments, but their clothes were brightly coloured and often decorated with embroidered designs. Men wore loincloths of wool, leather or linen, fastened by tight belts. Women wore full, flounced skirts and close-fitting jackets.

Cloaks and tunics

On the Greek mainland, the everyday dress for men was a knee-length chiton (tunic), made of woollen fabric seamed or pinned at the shoulders and the sides. In cold weather, a chamlys (short cloak) or himation (long cloak) was worn on top. Old men, and men in authority, often wore long tunics that reached to the ground.

This young Cretan serving man, left, is wearing a close-fitting loincloth with a fish-scale pattern and a wide decorative border.

Graceful and comfortable

Greek women's clothes were made in a similar way to men's, from long, unstructured lengths of cloth. The most common women's garment was the peplos, made by pinning a length of cloth at the shoulders, then binding it close to the body by a girdle (band of braid or ribbon) tied round the waist and below the breasts. Outside the home, Greek women wore a himation (cloak) as well, and used part of it to cover their heads and faces.

Did you know...?

Greeks wove each length of cloth specially for the person who would wear it to ensure that their clothes would fit.

Greek farmers dressed in traditional himations.

A young Spartan woman athlete, dressed only in a short tunic.

Uncovered

Greek men often went naked, especially when working in a hot environment. A fit and healthy body was admirable, and likely to be the home of a good or noble soul. In contrast, respectable Greek women wore long clothes that covered most of their bodies. But the city-state of Sparta was famous for the freedom given to its women and for the short, man-like clothes they wore.

THE ANCIENT GREEK WORLD

The Ancient Greeks believed that the head was the home of the soul. Greek head coverings displayed the wearer's moral worth, as well as having practical uses. Greek people also travelled widely, learning leather-working and shoe-making technologies from neighbouring peoples.

Greek Men

Many Greek men went bare-headed for most of the time. As citizens of democratic states, they felt proud and free, with nothing to hide. When it rained, they wore a pesatos (wide brimmed leather hat) or pulled their cloaks over their head. Athletes tied their hair back with ribbons, to keep it out of their eyes.

Greek Women

Greek men expected respectable women to cover their hair with veils. Beneath these veils, women arranged their long hair in elaborate braids, curls and buns. Women's hairstyles were held in place by coloured scarves or ribbons, and decorated with jewelled hairpins or diadems (headbands). Ancient Greek jewellers were highly skilled at working with gold.

Did you know...?

The prize given to the first Olympic champions was a garland of leaves from holy trees.

A gold diadem to be worn in a woman's hair, from the island of Milos, dated 300 BC.

Rough country

In wartime, Greek warriors protected their legs with curved greaves (shin-plates). These were made of metal (for rich men) or thick boiled leather (for ordinary soldiers). They fastened behind the leg with leather straps and buckles, and were worn with short lace-up boots or heavy sandals.

Female fashions

Greek footwear was made from soft leather, smoothed and polished with pork fat or olive oil. It was often brightly coloured with plant dyes. For women, fashionable styles included slippers, open-toed shoes, mules (shoes without heel-backs), shoes with thick cork soles and sandals.

A marble female foot dressed in a sandal, dating from 1st-2nd century AD.

This statue of Asclepius, the Greek god of medicine, shows him wearing sturdy ankle boots with thick soles and open toes.

Styles for men

Greek men also wore sandals. But for long journeys, they put on walking shoes with thick, hobnailed soles, or short lace-up boots that protected the foot and gave extra support to the ankles.

THE ANCIENT GREEK WORLD

Greek civilisation has been influenced by traditions from Asia and Europe since the first people appeared 5,000 years ago. It was also one of the first places in Europe to develop its own distinctive culture and jewellery.

Treasure from Troy

Some of the finest Ancient Greek poetry describes a war between the Greeks and the Trojans, who lived in western Asia. There were also peaceful, trading, contacts between Greek and Trojan people; trade goods included fabrics, foodstuffs, and gold. Trojan jewellery was made of pure sheet gold, cut, hammered or engraved to create earrings, necklaces, pendants and diadems. Its West Asian styles and techniques influenced Greek craftworkers for many hundreds of years.

Oiled skins, pale faces

This gold necklace was found at Troy and was probably made around 2000 BC.

Traditional Greek jugs such as this one were often used to carry olive oil.

The Greeks admired natural, healthy bodies. Men and women bathed regularly in clean water, and then rubbed olive oil (one of Ancient Greece's main products) into their skin and hair. This had a smoothing and softening effect, and eased painful sunburn. Greek men did not wear make-up, but Greek women use simple cosmetics, such as soot, crushed earth and herbs, all mixed with olive oil, to colour their lips, cheeks and eye-lids.

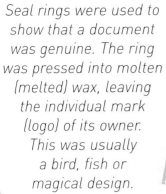

Seal rings were used to show that a document was genuine. The ring was pressed into molten (melted) wax, leaving the individual mark (logo) of its owner. This was usually a bird, fish or magical design.

Myths and legends

From around 500 BC to around 350 BC, Greece was at war. Citizens spent money on weapons, not on jewellery. Jewels were still made, but only a few were of precious gold. These used filigree (twisted wire) techniques, plus old-style hammering and engraving. But after around 350 BC, Greek craftworkers made magnificent bracelets, necklaces, pendants and earrings. Most featured polished precious stones, braids of twisted gold wire, and life-like details from nature. Decorations included tiny moulded scenes from Greek myths and legends.

This section of richly-tattooed skin was taken from a Central Asian princess/warrior buried in frozen ground around 200 BC.

Tattoos

The Greeks were proud of their culture and their language. They called people who could not speak it 'barbarians'. The Greeks were shocked by 'barbarian' body-ornament traditions, even though tattooing was practiced by their northern neighbours, the Scythians, and by the Uighur people who lived on the vast Central Asian plains. The Greeks tattooed slaves who worked in their homes to stop them running away, but were shocked at the thought of tattooing free Greek citizen bodies.

THE ROMAN EMPIRE

The Romans' home in central Italy was close to Ancient Greek lands. Like Greek clothes, early Roman garments were just lengths of fabric, folded to fit the body. But towards the end of the Roman era clothes styles began to change, as the Romans learned new designs and techniques from peoples they ruled.

The toga

The earliest Roman garment was the toga. Originally, it was the only piece of clothing Roman men and women wore, but by around 200 BC, it had become a sign of Roman citizenship, and was restricted to men only. Each toga was a huge, heavy woollen cloak, shaped like a half circle. It was made by trimming away the lower corners from a long rectangle of cloth.

A Roman soldier dressed in a short tunic, ideal for easy movement.

Ready for work

A long, heavy toga made it difficult for the wearer to move quickly or do hard physical work. So, from around 200 BC, most ordinary Roman men – and slaves - wore short tunics, similar to the Greek chiton. Underneath, they wore a loincloth; on top, when it was cold, they wore a blanket or a short, hooded cloak.

"Barberini Man Wearing a Toga", carrying busts of two ancestors (Centrale Montemartini, Capitoline Museums).

The layered look

Roman women also wore tunics, but floor-length, draped, and tied with decorative girdles. Often, they wore two or more tunics at the same time. Eventually, the outer tunic became known as a stola. Women wore a long cloak, called a palla, over their tunics and sometimes a veil. Women's underwear included a lightweight loincloth and a supportive band of cloth around the breasts, called a mammilare.

Women's tunics were pinned at the shoulder and tied round the waist.

Did you know...?
The average Roman toga was about 5.5 m along its straight edge and 1.7 m at its widest point.

Trousers worn by a Celtic warrior dating from 500 BC. They were popular in north-west Europe, and with Central Asian nomad tribes.

'Barbarian' clothes

At its peak, the Roman empire stretched from the border of Scotland to Syria. Romans considered anyone who wasn't from Rome to be a 'Barbarian'. Such peoples living in conquered lands wore many different styles of clothing. Some were made from draped lengths of fabric, like the Romans' own. But others, such as trousers, were cut from woven fabric in shaped, separate sections, then carefully stitched together. After around AD 100, the Romans slowly began to copy them.

THE ROMAN EMPIRE

The Ancient Romans inherited many fashions from their neighbours in Greece. But the Romans also followed old Italian customs, and invented new traditions of their own. Late Roman styles were influenced by contact with Germanic and Celtic peoples from north-west Europe from the 3rd century BC. These people had their own typical head coverings and hats.

Women's veils

A Roman bride with her veil turned back.

Like the Greeks, Roman women wore veils. They chose different colours and styles for different occasions. Flame-red veils were for weddings to scare evil spirits away. With their veils, brides wore garlands of wild flowers and a complicated cone-shaped hairstyle.

Garlands

Roman emperors wore garlands, but of laurel leaves, not flowers. Roman generals were 'crowned' with laurel as they marched in triumphant processions. Roman writers suggested several reasons for these customs. Laurel represented peace, joy and victory. As an evergreen tree, with leaves all year round, it was a symbol of undying strength. It was also sacred to Jupiter, the most powerful Roman god.

Roman coins were stamped with portraits of reigning emperors crowned with laurel leaves.

Did you know...?
Wigs of blonde or bleached hair, cut from German and Baltic captives, started a new Roman fashion.

Beards and 'big hair'

Roman hairstyles also changed over the centuries. In the early years of Roman power, men wore close-cropped hair and were clean shaven. Women's hair was tied in a neat bun at the back of the head, or bound with a scarf in Greek style. But after around AD 200, beards and curls became fashionable for men, while women wore elaborate styles that required specially-trained slaves to arrange them. Curls, braids and rolls of hair surrounded the face or were piled on top of the head, like a crown.

'Big hair' around 200 BC. To achieve favourite styles, natural hair was padded with sheep's wool or long locks of human hair.

Northern fashions

By around AD 100, Rome ruled a large part of north-western Europe. The Celtic and German peoples living there all dressed in their own local styles. These featured woollen cloaks, tunics and trousers for men; the most fashionable had checked patterns. Northern women wore long woollen skirts, topped by short jackets or belted tunics, plus long cloaks fastened by large metal brooches. Hair fashions for men and women included bleaching (to create red or golden tresses) plus short, spiky haircuts – and moustaches – for warriors, and long flowing locks for women.

Celtic Queen Boudicca (c. AD 50) was known for her colourful woollen garments.

THE ROMAN EMPIRE

The Ancient Romans were rich and powerful. They ruled an empire that stretched from Scotland to Syria – and wore more jewellery than anyone had ever done before. Jewellery workers moved to Rome from distant parts of the empire. Gold, silver and precious stones were carried there by victorious armies and long-distance traders.

Wonderful work

Roman jewellery styles were based on designs and techniques copied from the Ancient Greeks and from the Etruscans, who lived in Italy before Rome grew powerful. Etruscan goldsmiths were extremely skilful. Their finest works include brooches decorated with tiny animals and patterned with granulation (rows of metal balls around 0.03 cm in diameter).

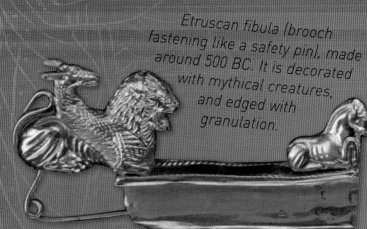

Etruscan fibula (brooch fastening like a safety pin), made around 500 BC. It is decorated with mythical creatures, and edged with granulation.

Precious metals

The Romans liked their jewellery to be made of gold. But Roman metal-workers also produced decorative beauty-care tools in silver and bronze. Mirrors, dishes and hairpins were carved, or cast in moulds, to create raised patterns, or engraved (scratched with a sharp point) to produce a surface design. Roman shopkeepers often used metals to make cosmetic mixtures, such as white lead face powder. It created a fashionable pale complexion (suntan was for slaves) – but, in large quantities, it could kill!

This bronze Roman mirror is engraved with a picture of a loving couple, drinking wine. It has a handle so that a slave could hold it up in front of her mistress' face.

Shoes and socks

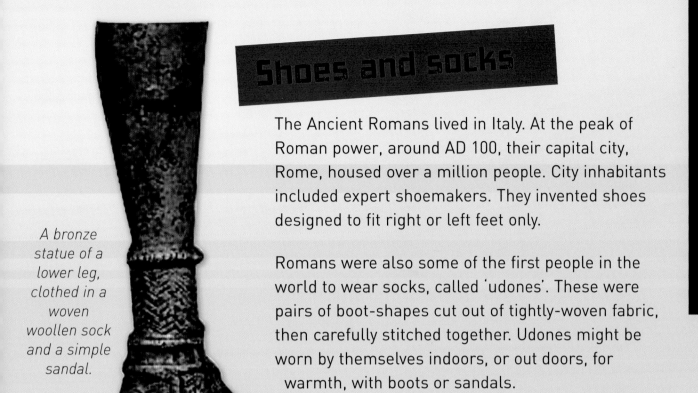

A bronze statue of a lower leg, clothed in a woven woollen sock and a simple sandal.

The Ancient Romans lived in Italy. At the peak of Roman power, around AD 100, their capital city, Rome, housed over a million people. City inhabitants included expert shoemakers. They invented shoes designed to fit right or left feet only.

Romans were also some of the first people in the world to wear socks, called 'udones'. These were pairs of boot-shapes cut out of tightly-woven fabric, then carefully stitched together. Udones might be worn by themselves indoors, or out doors, for warmth, with boots or sandals.

Did you know...?

The Romans used the outer rinds of pomegranates, dried and imported from Asia, to dye their leather shoes red.

Caligae and Calcaei

For outdoor wear, the most important foot coverings were caligae (shoes or boots with thick, hobnailed soles made of many layers of leather) and calcaei (flat leather shoes, shaped like ballet shoes). Calcaei could only be worn by high-ranking Romans.

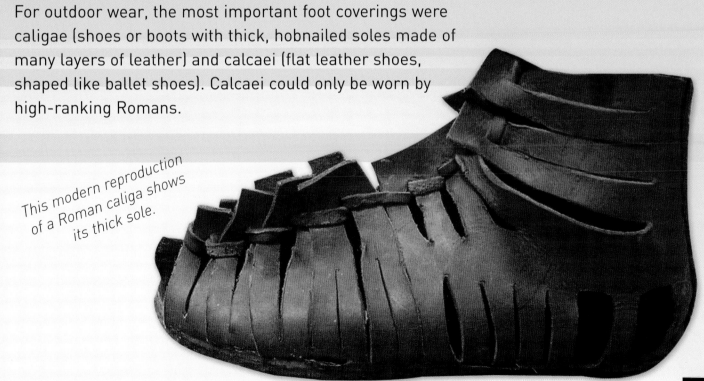

This modern reproduction of a Roman caliga shows its thick sole.

MEDIEVAL EUROPE

The medieval period started around AD 500. At that time, people in southern Europe wore similar clothes to old Roman fashions. But slowly, new ways of making clothes were invented. These created dramatically new styles.

Typical tunics

This 11th century illustration shows a wine seller dressed in a typical tunic of the time.

In Europe, a T-shaped tunic remained the standard male garment. It was cut and sewn in a neater, less bulky shape than in previous centuries. It now had long sleeves, for warmth, belted round the waist, and worn with a thick cloak. In northern Europe, men also wore baggy trousers.

Surcoats and wimples

Early medieval women wore long, loose tunic-shaped dresses, sewn with side seams, and with long wide sleeves. Underneath, they wore a long chemise (loosely fitting dress). On top, they often wore a sleeveless surcoat (over-dress), cut and sewn in different regional designs, plus a heavy woollen cloak in winter weather. Married women covered their hair with scarves, veils or wimples (a wide band of cloth, hiding the neck and reaching up to the chin).

This Viking woman, from around AD 1050, is wearing a long tunic topped by a two-piece overdress.

Did you know...?

Tight-fitting clothing required the invention of adjustable fastenings — otherwise fitted styles would have been impossible to put on.

Dull colours

Everyday clothes, worn by ordinary people, began to be made in these new, fitted styles. But, unlike bright, patterned clothes, worn by the rich, they only appeared in plain colours. This was because ordinary people could not afford exotic imported fabrics, or expensive coloured dyes. Their everyday clothes were made from rough homespun wool or linen, in natural shades of cream, grey, brown or coloured with muted, earthy plant dyes.

A north-European family, around AD 1480, wearing stylishly shaped, but dull-coloured clothing.

The explorer Sir Walter Raleigh often wore an extravagantly tailored outfit.

Figure display

Towards the end of the medieval period, new ways of tailoring allowed clothes to fit much more closely. Fashions that revealed body shapes became very popular among rich young men and women. Female clothes featured low, scooped necklines, narrow sleeves, tight waists, and skirts that flared outwards from the hips to the floor. Fashionable men wore short, tight doublets (fitted tunics) with wide shoulders and narrow waists, together with pointed shoes and clinging hose (separate stockings for each leg, cut and sewn from cloth).

MEDIEVAL EUROPE

After AD 500, Roman-style jewellery remained popular throughout southern Europe. But in the north and east, it was replaced by local, non-Roman designs. For a while, women – and men – continued to wear make-up. But the fast-growing Christian Church taught that cosmetics were sinful. By AD 1000, face and body paint were out of favour in all Christian lands.

Saxons and Vikings

In Britain, Germany and Scandinavia, jewellers created magnificent brooches of gold, silver and bronze. These were designed to be useful – they fastened cloaks and other clothing – but also to impress. Anglo-Saxon jewellery was decorated with braided wire or filigree (lacy, twisted) metal, plus polished precious stones and brightly-coloured enamel (layers of glass). Viking jewellers preferred solid metal shaped by hammering, twisting, carving and casting techniques.

Charms, necklaces, rings

This Viking necklace was made of carefully-shaped amber beads, probably around AD 900. The original bead-string has rotted away.

Favourite Viking designs included amulets (lucky charms, often shaped like the god Thor's hammer), and huge, heavy, metal necklaces and arm-rings. These were often given to warriors by Viking chiefs as a reward for bravery in battle. Viking jewellery for women featured large round or oval brooches, and necklaces strung with imported treasures: glass beads from Germany, Arab coins from West Asia, and amber from the eastern shores of the Baltic Sea.

Christian symbols

After around AD 1000, medieval jewellery was often made in the shape of Christian symbols, or decorated with portraits of holy saints. But medieval people also liked jewellery in non-religious designs. They wore souvenir pins to show that they had travelled to distant places, and heraldic badges to display their ancestry, or loyalty to their lord. They also gave and wore jewellery as a sign of love.

Early medieval brooch from Pen-y-Corddyn Mawr hillfort, near Abergele, Wales, 8th century.

Jewelled clothes

By the end of the medieval period, around AD 1500, rich peoples' clothes were trimmed with real gold and silver embroidery. Wealthy women wore girdles decorated with pearls; powerful men dressed in jewel-studded buckles and heavy gold chains. Ordinary people could not afford such luxury. Instead, they added cheap iron pins and brooches to their clothes.

This tapestry (wall-hanging) was woven in Flanders (now Belgium) around AD 1500. It shows two wealthy women wearing jewellery and richly-jewelled clothes.

Did you know...?

Some people in the medieval period thought Bezoar stones — a natural substance found in the digestive system of goats — would protect their wearers from the plague. They didn't work.

MEDIEVAL EUROPE

After Roman power weakened soon after AD 300, the empire's lands were divided among many different peoples. New languages, customs and designs for headgear evolved. Because different peoples settled in different parts of Europe, their clothing developed into distinctive regional styles.

Local headgear

Local climate and farming practices influenced ordinary people's headgear. Married women throughout medieval Europe continued to cover their heads with veils or shawls, but men's hats varied widely. In hot, sunny Italy, for example, men's hats had wide shady brims. In cold, snowy lands, like Viking Russia and Scandinavia, men made hats of bushy fox-fur. In wet, windy Britain, they continued to wear Celtic-style hoods.

This Italian farm-worker is wearing a wide-brimmed hat made from locally-grown wheat-straw, plaited then stitched together.

An illustration from a 15th-century Dutch calendar showing women wearing elaborately horned hats.

Women's hats

Around the same time, rich women began to wear hats, instead of simple veils. At first, their hats were based on male designs. But after around AD 1400, women's fashions included tall, pointed hennins (steeple-hats), wide, padded hats with horns, and 'gable' headdresses that formed a pointed frame around the face to wear Celtic-style hoods.

Leg Protection

Ordinary men and women, who worked on the land, needed protection from the cold and damp, and from rough vegetation. They could not afford socks, or high leather boots that reached to the knee. So they wore simple flat shoes, and protected their lower legs with bands of cloth or sheep skin.

Did you know...?

The points on medieval men's shoes could be up to 6 inches long.

High fashion

Wealthy men and women wore many different styles of fine leather shoes, with shapes that changed over the centuries. Many popular designs had long, pointed toes, stuffed with sheep's wool for stiffening. By around AD 1400, fine shoes worn outside the home were protected by 'pattens' – thick over-shoes, rather like clogs, made of wood and leather.

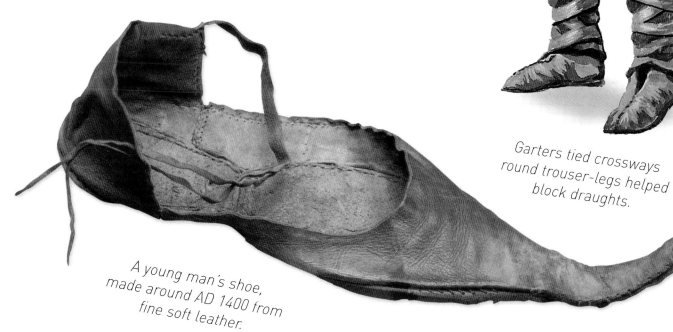

Garters tied crossways round trouser-legs helped block draughts.

A young man's shoe, made around AD 1400 from fine soft leather.

EASTERN REGIONS

Throughout most of Asia, ordinary people in the past worked outside as farmers, growing crops on the land, or tended flocks of sheep and cattle. Their everyday clothes had to protect them from extreme weather conditions.

Loose and cool

Men from Algeria wore traditional robes to protect them from sunburn.

In many parts of West Asia, men and women wore long, loose, flowing tunics, with wide sleeves. On top, they wore a robe which was given names such as jubba. They were simply made, from lengths of cloth stitched together without tailoring. Fabrics included cotton, linen and wool.

It's a wrap!

In India, ancient styles based on lengths of fabric wrapped around the body, continued to prove useful for thousands of years. Indian women folded and draped long lengths of cloth into graceful saris. Indian men wore a dhoti, a rectangle of cloth that could be wrapped like a skirt, or wound between the legs to create loose, baggy trousers. Similar styles developed in south-east Asia, where they were worn by men and women, and called sarongs. There were many other regional variations too.

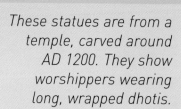
These statues are from a temple, carved around AD 1200. They show worshippers wearing long, wrapped dhotis.

Dragon robes

In China, the right to wear different kinds of clothing was controlled by law. Men from the ruling class were allowed to dress in long, heavy robes. From AD 1391, Chinese mandarins (royal officials) added large square emblems to display their rank. Emperors had a picture of a dragon, the symbol of the Chinese empire, on their robes.

Chinese workers

Traditionally, ordinary Chinese people wore long, wrap-fronted robes, or short, front-fastening jackets. Both styles were tied with a sash around the waist, and were paired with long cotton or linen skirts or loose trousers. But when Manchu invaders from the north conquered China in AD 1644, they forced Chinese workers to wear clothes similar to Manchu styles. These included long, loose robes with wide sleeves and high collars.

Did you know...?
Chinese workers kept themselves warm by wearing jackets padded with thick layers of cotton wadding.

This elaborate 14th-century samurai armour, was made for ceremonial occasions.

Chinese influence

Japanese and Korean fashions were often influenced by designs from China. Soon after AD 700, traditional Japanese clothes (a short jacket over trousers or a skirt) were replaced by a long Chinese-style robe, later known in Japanese as a kimono. For centuries, it was fashionable for Japanese women to wear many layers of thin, fine kimono robes. The edges of the sleeves and neckline were carefully adjusted, so that layers of contrasting colours could be displayed.

EASTERN REGIONS

The peoples of Asia created many different kinds of footwear. Designs were shaped by local climates, and by available materials. Wars, invasions and migrations also brought changes of footwear.

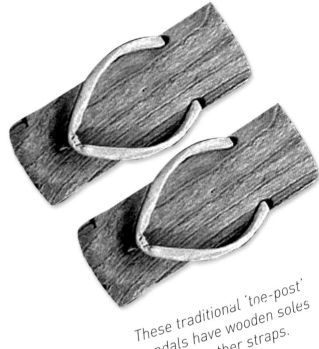

These traditional 'toe-post' sandals have wooden soles and leather straps.

Central Asian boots

The Mughal dynasty, who ruled north India from AD 1526 to 1858, were descended from Mongol princes. This painting shows typical Central-Asian style boots.

In many parts of East Asia, outdoor footwear styles were based on soft leather ankle boots worn by nomads who rode on horseback across grassy steppes. From around AD 1200 – 1500 these styles were carried over a vast area, from China to India and Russia, by armies of Mongol invaders. Indoors, men and women went barefoot, or wore backless slippers. These were also popular in West Asia.

Simple sandals

In hot tropical regions, for example, South-East Asia, many people went barefoot or wore simple, lightweight sandals. These were made of wood, leather or plaited plant fibres. Typically, they had straps running along each side of the foot from a small 'post' in between the toes.

Kip·kap and geta

For protection from rain, or from rubbish in the streets, women in many parts of Asia wore clogs with thick wooden soles that raised their feet at least 5 cm above dirty ground. These clogs often had names that echoed the sound the wearer made as she clattered along. In Turkey they were called 'kip-kap' (or 'kub-kob'), in Japan 'geta'.

This Japanese woman and her servant girl wear wooden geta clogs with 'tabi' (socks that have a separate space for the big toe).

Did you know...?

The Chinese poet Xie Lingyin, invented the first non-slip footwear around 350 BC.

Tiny shoes and 'lily feet'

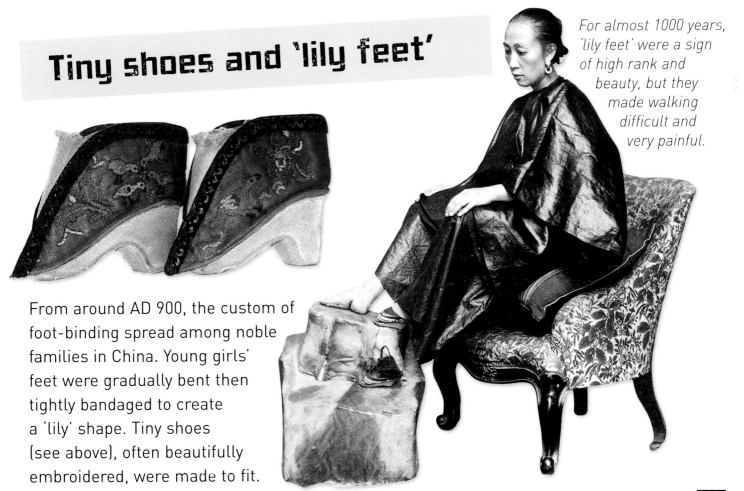

For almost 1000 years, 'lily feet' were a sign of high rank and beauty, but they made walking difficult and very painful.

From around AD 900, the custom of foot-binding spread among noble families in China. Young girls' feet were gradually bent then tightly bandaged to create a 'lily' shape. Tiny shoes (see above), often beautifully embroidered, were made to fit.

EASTERN REGIONS

Many different peoples of Asia all had their own customs and traditions, which were reflected in their clothes. They lived in many environments, and followed several of the world's great faiths. These factors also affected what they chose to wear.

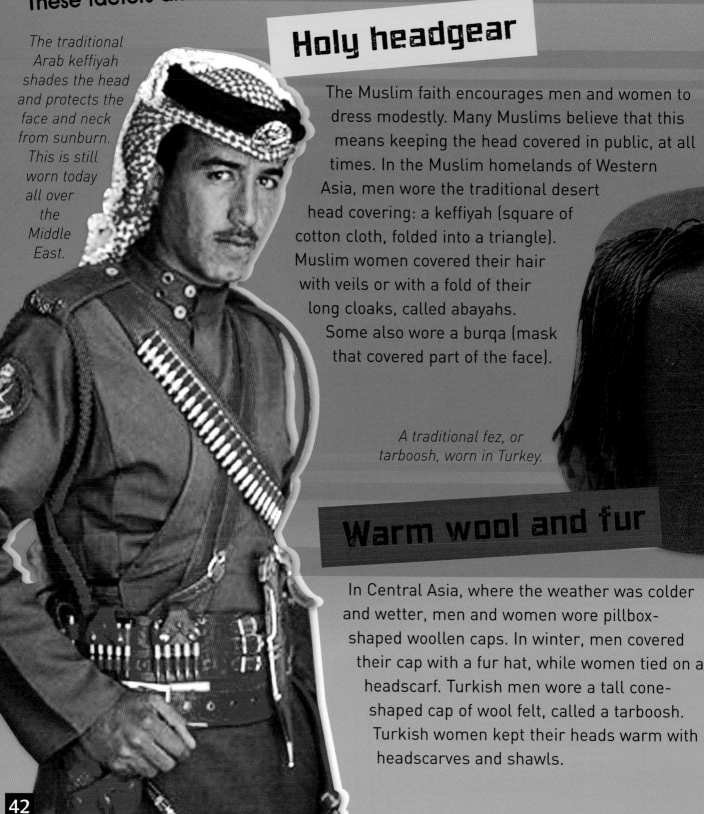

The traditional Arab keffiyah shades the head and protects the face and neck from sunburn. This is still worn today all over the Middle East.

Holy headgear

The Muslim faith encourages men and women to dress modestly. Many Muslims believe that this means keeping the head covered in public, at all times. In the Muslim homelands of Western Asia, men wore the traditional desert head covering: a keffiyah (square of cotton cloth, folded into a triangle). Muslim women covered their hair with veils or with a fold of their long cloaks, called abayahs. Some also wore a burqa (mask that covered part of the face).

A traditional fez, or tarboosh, worn in Turkey.

Warm wool and fur

In Central Asia, where the weather was colder and wetter, men and women wore pillbox-shaped woollen caps. In winter, men covered their cap with a fur hat, while women tied on a headscarf. Turkish men wore a tall cone-shaped cap of wool felt, called a tarboosh. Turkish women kept their heads warm with headscarves and shawls.

Pillboxes and turbans

In many parts of India and South-East Asia, turbans (long strips of cloth wound round the head) were the usual headgear for men. Women draped a fold of their sari (wrapped cloth robe) or a long, wide dupatta (headscarf) over their hair. For work in the rice-fields, farmers throughout South-East Asia made shady, waterproof hats of tough local materials, such as bamboo or woven palm-fronds.

Muslim scholars dressed in turbans around AD 1350. Many Muslims and Sikhs still wear turbans today.

'Shaking when walking'

In China, jewellery was traditionally sewn on to clothes. Chinese jewels included hooks and buckles made from bone, ivory and bronze, and pins to fasten women's long hair. These often had jingling pendants attached, so were known as pu yao 'shaking when walking'. Traditional Chinese jewellery did not feature precious stones – except for smooth green jade, the symbol of wisdom, courage and long life. This was carved into beads and decorative plaques, and sewn onto clothing.

Two-pronged Chinese hairpins, made of delicate cut and twisted silver around AD 800.

Did you know...?
In Western countries a tarboosh is usually called a fez.

Holy signs, precious stones

Many of the world's finest gems were found in India. Worn in large quantities by rich women, they often covered the body like a second skin. Married Hindu women – and holy men – wore a red dot on the forehead. This is said to be the site of a mystical 'third eye' that brought spiritual understanding. For good luck and happiness, Muslim brides covered their hands and feet with henna patterns before their weddings.

AFRICA

In most of Africa, the climate was warm all year round. The land was covered with dense rainforest, or tall grasses and thorn bushes. Most men and women led very active lives, and tight, complicated clothes would have stopped them from travelling far or working. Children often went naked for the first few years of life.

Bark and leather

Leather garments were often decorated with fringes, strips of animal fur, or beads.

The earliest African clothes were made of natural substances. For example, in southern and east-central Africa, leather from hunted animals, or specially treated tree-bark, was made into aprons. These were worn in pairs, at the front and the back of the body, by men and unmarried girls. Married women wore a leather skirt and cloak instead.

Wrapped cloth

The first woven cloth in Africa was made around 3000 BC. Over the centuries, African weavers became very skillful at spinning thread from wool, goat hair, or plant fibres such as raffia, dying it in brilliant colours, and weaving it into cloth. They also obtained rough silk thread by unwrapping African moth cocoons. Most garments were not cut or sewn, but just draped and tied around the body. Wrapped styles included simple blanket-cloaks, worn by East African cattle-herders, and white wrap-around robes, worn in Ethiopia.

East-African cloak. Fastened at the shoulder, it leaves both hands free for work.

Robes and slings

In crop-growing and trading communities, especially in West Africa, wrapped clothes became more elaborate as individual wealth increased and people could afford more fabric. Successful men wore full wrap-around robes draped in impressive, dignified styles. New designs for men appeared, such as the tunic made from a length of folded cloth with an opening for the head. West African women wore long wrapped skirts or full-length wrap dresses. They also wound lengths of cloth around their backs to carry young babies in.

A Nigerian wearing a traditional expansive tunic.

Modest and practical

In North Africa, harsh desert conditions made nakedness uncomfortable. Long robes, for men and women, were cooler and more airy. After around AD 700, a new religion made covering the body essential for most North African people. They converted to Islam, which teaches that both men and women should be modestly dressed.

North African robes were made from a long length of fabric, folded in two, and left partly open on either side of the body. The openings served as sleeves, and provided coolness.

Muslim soldiers from Asia also brought new styles with them, especially trousers. These became everyday wear under long, loose robes, for many North African men. North African women also wore long robes, topped by cloaks and wide, gauzy scarves or veils.

AFRICA

In many parts of Africa, the traditional fashion was nudity – especially for younger people. According to ancient local beliefs, this was a sign of dignity and purity. As adult men and women grew richer, they added extra clothes and splendid jewellery.

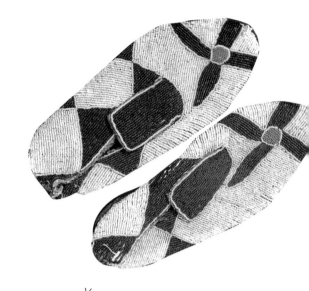

Yoruba royal boots and shoes were richly decorated with coloured beads that covered their entire surface.

Fit for a king

Footwear was expensive, and therefore became a status symbol. It also featured in several traditional rituals. For example, kings of the Asanti people (now of Ghana, West Africa) were never meant to set foot on the ground. They were too important and too holy. They were carried everywhere by their servants, and their feet were protected by special shoes. Other West African rulers, such as kings of the Yoruba people (now of Nigeria, West Africa) also wore fancy footwear, as signs of their special status.

An official from Ghana wears a fine locally woven 'kente' cloth. The cloth is still worn today by Asanti people.

Fine fabrics

Kente cloth was woven in narrow strips and brilliant colours and patterns. It was originally made by the Asanti people for their kings, but became popular with fashionable people throughout West Africa. Each colour had a special meaning: gold stood for high rank, green represented re-birth, red symbolised power and passion, blue brought harmony and yellow meant fertility. Black was the colour of seriousness and spirituality.

Did you know...?
African mud-cloth gets its name from coloured earths and other natural dyes used to make it.

Power and prestige

In West Africa, two popular styles of draping cloth were Kyere W'anantu (Show your Legs) in which cloth was wrapped round the body from the shoulders to the knees, and Okatakyie (Brave Man), which covered the body from chest to calf, and featured a long length of cloth draped over one arm. The first style was favoured by strong, active, athletic men who wished to show off their bodies. The second, which looked dignified and impressive, was usually worn by chiefs.Women draped cloth to create skirts, shawls and elaborate geles (head-ties). The larger and more complicated the head ties, the higher the woman's status.

A Nigerian woman in a traditional head-tie.

Fashions from overseas

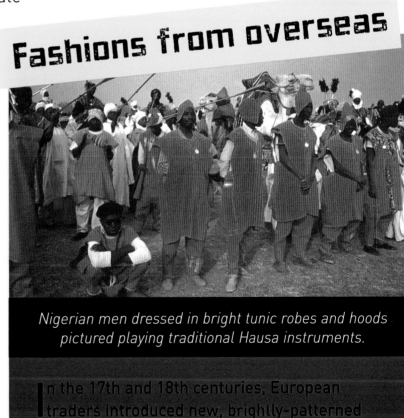

Nigerian men dressed in bright tunic robes and hoods pictured playing traditional Hausa instruments.

In the 17th and 18th centuries, European traders introduced new, brightly-patterned 'batik' cloths. These were originally made in Asia, but were copied and mass-produced in Europe for export to Africa. Traders from Europe and Asia also introduced new clothing styles, based on robes or shirts and trousers. Both became fashionable, especially in West Africa, and were copied and changed by African craftworkers to suit local tastes and conditions.

AFRICA

Traditionally, African men and women wore a wide range of headgear. It was made in different styles and materials, depending on the local environment and resources. African hairstyles followed traditional local designs, each with their own meaning. Typically, styles included braids, hairpins, decorative combs, feathers and coloured clay.

Traditionally, the Tuareg men of Morocco wore veils dyed deep blue with indigo. In Sudan, white veils were popular.

Dressed for the desert

Men and women living in or around the vast, sandy Sahara Desert needed headgear that would protect them from heat, dust, sandstorms and sunburn. So they covered their heads, and the lower part of their faces, with long strips of cloth, wound round and round. Men's styles looked rather like a turban, with a wide cloth strip protecting the mouth and nose. Women's styles were simpler, rather like shawls, and covered the whole face.

Beautiful beads

The first glass beads in Africa were made by the Ancient Egyptians, over 3000 years ago. Beads were used for decoration. Often, they carried a special meaning. Among the Masai people (now in Kenya, East Africa), the number of bead necklaces a woman wore showed whether she was married or not, how many children she had, and how rich her family was.

Signs of belonging

Many hats were worn, by men and women, to display their membership of one particular group. Sometimes, headgear was a sign of tribal or national identity. For example, the Herero women of Namibia wore high, wide hats, called 'duk', made of tightly-wrapped cloth. Sometimes,

Herero women from Namibia in traditional duk hats.

headgear displayed rank or bravery. Warriors from the Zulu people of South Africa wore plumes of ostrich feathers, and Masai warriors coloured their hair with orange mud and arranged it in plaits. Often, headdresses were an important part of ceremonial costumes, worn by masked dancers and priests.

Paint and patterns

Ordinary African people could not afford precious metals; they made necklaces, belts and bracelets from leather, bone and stone. They also created striking designs for painting bodies and faces. Body paint was mostly worn when taking part in special ceremonies, for example, to announce that a young boy or girl had passed from childhood to adult status. Scarification (patterns of scars made on the skin) displayed membership of a warrior brotherhood or powerful family clan.

This village elder from Sudan is shown wearing the traditional scarification across the forehead with a mud paste.

49

THE AMERICAS

Early humans first reached Alaska, in the far north of America, some time before 35,000 BC. Slowly, they spread southwards, reaching the tip of South America by around 9000 BC. Different groups settled in separate localities, and developed their own styles of clothing for everyday wear.

Soft warm fleece

Clothes from the Americas were made from materials that were available locally. These varied widely from place to place. Some were found only in the Americas. In the high Andes Mountains region, Inca women wove ponchos (thick cloaks like blankets, with a hole for the head) from the fleece of native llama and alpaca, dyed in vivid colours. Ponchos were worn by men over knee-length tunics, woven from plant fibres. Inca women wore loose, straight-sided ankle-length dresses.

Pelts and furs

In icy Arctic regions of North America, Inuit and Aleut peoples made clothes from the skins of animals they hunted for food: deer, caribou, polar bears, seals and foxes. These all had thick waterproof coats, that had evolved to help them survive in bitter weather. Arctic men and women all wore similar garments: a hooded tunic, called a parka or anorak, trousers and boots. In winter, they added extra tunics, called kuletak.

The Incas mummified dead bodies. They wrapped them in woven blankets and ponchos.

Skins, tails and paws

Other Native North Americans, also made clothes from animal skins. After cleaning them and softening them they sewed them together to make tunics for men or long dresses for women. At first, clothes-makers left the animals' manes, tails or paws in position as decoration. Later, they cut the skins to shape, and added colourful trimmings such as brightly-dyed porcupine quills.

This European portrait of an Inuit man from Alaska shows him dressed from head to toe in fur-lined clothes.

A woman's dress, made for the Sioux Native American people. The bodice is decorated with quills.

Did you know...?

The Inca people of South America called gold 'the sweat of the sun' and silver 'the tears of the moon'.

Settler styles

When the first Europeans arrived to settle in America, they brought clothes styles from their homelands with them. But their life in the 'New World' was harsh; many also disapproved of finery, for religious reasons. So they wore tough, hardwearing clothes, in dark, sober colours, made from extra-thick cloth and leather.

Settlers' clothes included tailored coats and knee-breeches for men, and long, full-skirted dresses for women.

THE AMERICAS

The vast continents of North and South America were home to many different peoples. All had their own traditions of dress, and their own special fashions and finery, but all fine clothes and jewels were strictly limited to rich, powerful people.

In South America, when important people died they were dressed in fine clothes and jewellery. They were then wrapped in specially-woven blankets or ponchos (cloaks), to make 'mummy-bundles', and placed in cool, dry caves or buried underground. In some cultures, for example, the Nazca of the Andes Mountains, children who were killed as sacrifices to mountain gods were dressed in finery, like mummies.

Did you know...?

The game known as lacrosse was invented by Native Americans who called it 'little brother war'.

A mummified head from the Nazca civilisation, Peru, 200 BC.

Feather fashions

Among the Aztec people, who lived in Central America, embroidered clothes and feather headdresses were top fashions for wealthy noblemen. Rich women wore embroidered clothes, as well. The finest feathers were collected as a tribute from conquered peoples or traded with rainforest hunters, and were treasured almost like gold. Lower grade feathers were also valuable. They were woven into cloaks, to create mobile, three-dimensional patterns, made into graceful hand-held fans, or glued on to warriors' shields. The Aztecs thought they gave magic protection.

This Aztec headdress, was worn by Aztec emperor Montezuma (died 1521).

52

Sporting gear

In many past civilisations, sport was a way of settling disputes between neighbouring communities. It was cheaper, quicker and less destructive than war. Games might last all day – or longer – with hundreds of men in each team. To take part, team members put on special finery. Typically, this included necklaces, body-paint, decorative belts and 'tails' made of coloured horsehair. These sports fashions showed which team they belonged to, and may also have been designed to give players good luck, speed and strength.

Caddo and Choctaw Native American tribes play baggataway, now known as lacrosse.

Colonial clothes

When the European settlers first arrived in North America, fashions differed from colony to colony for religious and practical reasons. In northern colonies, plain, simple clothing was preferred, and frivolous, 'ungodly', fashions were banned. Cold weather also made thick, stiff, heavy clothes necessary for survival. Further south, where the weather was warmer and religious attitudes more relaxed, clothes were lighter and more elaborate. After around AD 1700, these differences disappeared, as rich colonists all chose to follow the latest European fashions. In the earlier part of the century these styles were very elaborate. The biggest contrast in clothing was between smart, stylish town-dwellers and roughly-dressed country people.

A painting of George Washington by Charles Peele.

53

THE AMERICAS

The continents of North and South America provide some of the most extreme and varied environments on Earth. The Native peoples who lived there developed many different kinds of footwear, made from local materials.

Gold and feathers

In South America, the Inca peoples of the Andes mountains made boots of llama skin for protection against the cold. For Inca royalty, these might be covered with thin sheets of real silver or gold. Ordinary Aztec people went barefoot, or made sandals of cactus fibre. But Aztec warriors and nobles wore leather sandals decorated with feathers, and padded leather shin-guards in battle.

Aztec sandals fastened at the front of the foot with decorated laces.

Winter boots

Inuit and Aleut people lived in the far North of America, where the ground was frozen for most of the year, then boggy in the summer months. They made two different kinds of boots, plus indoor slippers of soft, furry hare skin. Winter boots were made of caribou skin or seal skin, hair side outwards. This produced a non-slip sole. Summer boots were made of thinner caribou skin. They were sewn with tiny stitches pulled very tight, to create waterproof seams.

Men's boots, made in Alaska, have seal skin soles and reindeer skin uppers, and are decorated with seal intestine, dog-hair, and wolverine fur.

Walking on Snow

In the cold northern regions of North America, native peoples made special shoes to allow them to hunt for food in the cold winter months, when deep snow covered the ground. Snow shoes have frames of wood or antler, with sinews or thin strips of leather laced across them. They spread the wearer's weight over a much wider area than the sole of a human foot, and prevented him from sinking into the snow. Snow shoes are still used today.

Native American hunters carrying bows and arrows and wearing snow shoes in different shapes.

Moccasins

Did you know...?

Native Americans softened animal hides by rubbing them with animal brains and fat before making them into shoes. Sometimes, women even chewed on them.

In the woodlands and grasslands of North America, shoes called 'Makisin' (now: 'moccasins') were made from single pieces of buck skin, gathered together around the top of the foot. The buck skin was used hair side inwards, to create a warm lining. Dry grass might also be packed inside, for extra insulation. Sometimes a flap was added to cover the upper instep, plus a wide cuff around the ankle.

These 19th century moccasins were made to a traditional design. They are decorated with bright glass beads, obtained by trading with European settlers.

EUROPE 1500-1750

After around AD 1500, clothing styles began to change more quickly in Europe. Clothes were very expensive however, so ordinary people still had to choose new garments for their hard-wearing qualities, as well as for their appearance. A new outfit was expected to last for at least 10 years.

Rich and poor

Wealthy people followed the latest fashions. In the 16th century, these featured tight corsets, stiffened skirts, trunk-hose (baggy shorts, fastened tightly round the thigh) and padded doublets (jackets). Ordinary peoples' clothes reflected fashionable shapes, but were looser and lighter. Men wore simple knee-length breeches, and women's skirts ended above the ankle.

Behind the times

In the 17th century, ordinary peoples' clothes continued to follow the fashion of the rich. Men's jackets became longer, covering the hips, and so did their trousers, which extended below the knee. Under their jackets, men wore a collarless shirt, and, often a sleeveless waistcoat. In some regions, like Highland Scotland, kilts (male skirts) were still worn. Ordinary women continued to wear long dresses with close-fitting bodices. Underneath, they wore a chemise and petticoats. For extra warmth, men and women wore cloaks; women also wore shawls.

These girls are dressed in the 16th century style. Their dresses (worn over long-sleeved chemises) have low square necks, narrow waists, and long, full skirts.

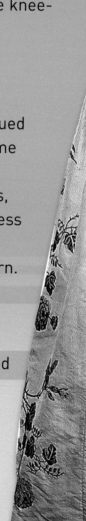

56

Revolutionary styles

Everyday clothes carried a political message, especially in 18th century France. Poor people, who often went hungry, were outraged to see the extravagant clothes worn by wealthy nobles. In return, rich politicians criticised the poor for being dressed in rags. French protesters, dressed in ordinary, everyday clothes, were nicknamed 'sans-culottes'. They did not wear – and could not afford – the fashionable, tailored knee-breeches (culottes).

Did you know...?
France was thought to be the most fashionable country in Europe in the 1700s

In 17th century Britain, fashionable royal courtiers wore clothes trimmed with ribbons, lace and bows. Ordinary people wore plainer styles.

Homespun clothes

Ordinary men and women could not afford expensive materials, such as lace, muslin (fine cotton), silk and velvet; they wore linen, hemp and wool. Often, cloth was woven from thread spun from local sheep's fleece by ordinary women, in their homes. They sold it to travelling merchants, who re-sold it to weavers in towns.

This early printed picture shows protesters attacking nobles in knee-breeches (left) and two poor people (far right) in ragged everyday clothes.

This fashionable silk dress, was worn by a wealthy noblewoman in around 1740.

EUROPE 1500-1750

After AD 1500, Europe changed fast. New contacts with the Americas, and with distant lands in Asia, challenged old certainties and brought new riches from trade. New ideas in art and literature, and political and religious differences were also reflected in European clothes styles.

Silk and damask

Around AD 1500, Italy was the European centre of fashion. Popes and Italian noble families ruled over brilliant courts. These rich, powerful Italians wore garments of silk and damask (a rich patterned fabric of cotton, linen, silk, or wool) imported from Asia. Noblemen wore new, short, fitted tunics, with close-fitting cloth stockings, topped by open-fronted robes. Noblewomen wore gowns with low, square necks.

Portrait of Guidubaldo II della Rovere, Duke of Urbino by Bartolomeo Passaroti (AD 1529-92).

Portrait of Queen Elizabeth I of England. She is wearing a jewelled robe with a long, tight 'stomacher' bodice and a wide ruff around her neck.

Spanish fashions

By around AD 1530, the colonies in South America made Spain the wealthiest and most fashionable nation. Spanish fashions were copied throughout Europe. Women's gowns had stiff, boned bodices (laced outer garments, worn like a vest over a blouse), and padded, bell-shaped skirts. Men's styles featured short, tight, padded doublets (jackets), baggy breeches, and knitted silk stockings.

Jewellery and art

Europe produced little gold and few precious stones. But, after AD 1500, European explorers reached lands where both could be found in large quantities. Ships brought Indian diamonds, Sri Lankan sapphires, Burmese rubies, Arabian pearls and South American emeralds, gold and silver back to Europe. Rich Europeans paid top artists and designers to create masterpieces for them. Jewels for women included long necklaces, hair ornaments, pendants and rings set with large precious stones. Men wore rings together with jewelled belts, collars and big medallions in their hats.

After around AD 1550, miniature portraits were set in gold and surrounded by jewels, and then worn on the chest like a brooch.

Portrait of King Louis XIV of France (reigned AD 1643 - 1715). He is wearing a very fashionable suit.

Dressed to impress

On state occasions, rival kings and princes all tried to display the most magnificent jewels. They also paid for artists to record their splendid appearance, weighed down by jewel-studded crowns, weapons, sceptres, miniature portraits and robes. For public appearances, women – and some men – wore make-up and rich, heavy perfumes.

After around AD 1500, the gap grew greater between elaborate new styles, worn by rich, high ranking people, and rough, simple shoes, worn for work by ordinary men and women. Men's footwear designs were more extreme than women's, since women's shoes were hidden by long, full skirts.

Boots and spurs

For most of the 17th century, Europe was at war. Fashions reflected military styles, such as long leather boots with thick sturdy soles and turn-over, 'bucket tops', originally designed to protect soldiers fighting on horseback. Underneath these tall boots, men wore over-the-knee stockings, trimmed at the top with lace or fringing that was designed to be seen. High-ranking men added spurs, a sign that they were officers, or knights.

Duck-bills

King Henry VIII of England (reigned AD 1509-1547) shown wearing embroidered silk square-toed shoes.

King Charles I (reigned AD 1625-1649) shown wearing 'bucket tops', footwear popular at the English royal court.

Medieval pointed shoes were replaced by shoes with extremely broad toes, nicknamed 'duck-bills'. They were often made of fragile luxury materials, such as silk or velvet. In the early 16th century, shoes might be slashed. This reflected high-fashion clothes worn by rich, powerful people.

This is an embroidered silk shoe with a sloping 'French' heel.

High heels

After around 1650, high heels became popular on boots, shoes and slippers worn by men and women. Heels first became popular in France, but soon spread to many parts of Europe. Heeled footwear was made of leather, silk and velvet. It might be decorated with gold or silver buckles, large ribbon rosettes or bows, or jewels and embroidery.

Did you know...?

'French' heels got their name because they were made popular by French kings who were of short stature.

Wooden clogs

Ordinary people could not afford high fashion footwear. Working men and women continued to wear plain ankle shoes, that had changed very little in design since the early Middle Ages. They also wore wooden pattens, or slip-on clogs. Both these styles were cheap, hard-working, and helped keep feet warm and dry when working on wet or frozen ground. With clogs, men and women wore thick knitted stockings, usually made from natural cream-coloured wool. Men sometimes also wore gaiters (shaped cloth leggings).

A couple from the Pyrénées Mountains in southern France. He is wearing traditional clogs; she wears plain, flat black-leather ankle shoes.

61

WESTERN WORLD 1750-1900

New inventions transformed everyday clothing after around AD 1750. Sewing machines meant that clothes could be stitched together much more quickly than before. Railways and cheap newspapers spread details of the latest fashions to ordinary people throughout Europe and the USA.

This dress, made of costly fabric, would have been worn by a wealthy woman around AD 1810.

Workwear and underwear

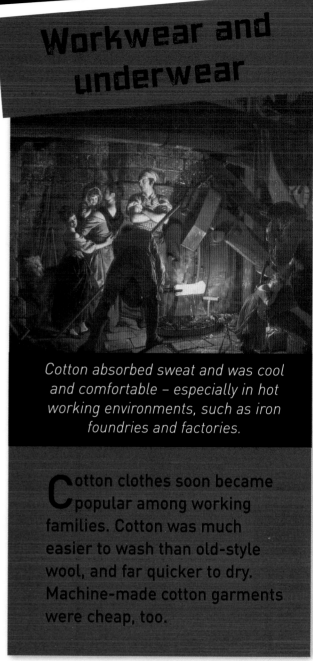

Cotton absorbed sweat and was cool and comfortable – especially in hot working environments, such as iron foundries and factories.

Cotton clothes soon became popular among working families. Cotton was much easier to wash than old-style wool, and far quicker to dry. Machine-made cotton garments were cheap, too.

Cotton for all

Originally, cotton was a rare, precious cloth, imported to Europe from India. But by the mid 19th century, new steamships carried vast quantities of raw cotton to European factories, where it was spun, woven and sewn on machines to make cheap clothing for everyday use. In the USA, cotton was grown on southern plantations worked by slaves, then sent to northern cities for processing.

Country traditions

This 19th-century farmworker is wearing a long-sleeved chemise, fitted bodice and full skirt.

Cotton was used to make tough clothes for male workers, such as full-length trousers and aprons, and also for men's shirts and underpants. For women, cotton cloth was sewn into blouses, camisoles (sleeveless tops, worn next to the skin), aprons, petticoats and knickers.

Before sewing machines were invented, cotton clothes were sewn by hand, usually in women's homes. In the countryside, working people continued to make many of their own everyday clothes by hand, using traditional materials and following traditional styles. But increasingly, they travelled to towns, to buy machine-made clothing there.

Did you know...?
The first sewing machines were called chain-stitch machines and were invented in 1858.

This picture from a fashion magazine shows the latest styles of women's dresses around 1900.

Fashion for all

By around 1900, cheap, machine-made garments, together with fashion magazines brought the latest styles closer to ordinary people. Women, especially, became much more fashion conscious. They wanted their everyday clothes to look up-to-date, yet still be practical to wear. So they looked for fashion details, such as high 'choker' necklines, when buying a sensible new outfit, or added fashionable trimmings, such as braid and lace, to existing everyday clothes.

WESTERN WORLD 1760-1900

During the 19th century, fashions for the rich changed more quickly than ever before, and fashionable styles were more elaborate. New businesses and industries created a new class of people with money to spend on lavish clothes, and opportunities for wearing them.

Napoleon's first wife, Empress Josephine, in a dress inspired by Ancient Greek fashion.

Greek revival

In the late 18th century, new political ideas, based on ancient Greek democracy, became fashionable in North America and France. Greece also inspired new women's fashions. From 1790 to 1815, fashionable dresses were long with high waists, but no other shaping. For evening wear, they were made of thin white cotton, to look like the drapery on Greeks statues. Modest women wore these dresses over flesh-coloured drawers (knickers), but ultra-fashionable women wore just one petticoat (a woman's slip or underskirt) underneath.

Corsets and crinolines

Around 1820, dresses, with corseted bodices, wide skirts and full sleeves became the new female fashion. They were worn with shapeless shawls and face-covering bonnets, plus layers of petticoats. By the 1850s, fashions were changing again thanks to new technology. Scientists created bright, permanent dyes, and engineers made steel springs for corsets and crinolines (vast hoop petticoats). For men, trousers were now paired with knee-length frock-coats (heavy overcoats).

A lady from the Victorian era wearing a tight corset.

Dress reform

Crinolines, corsets and bustles (frames worn under skirts to give them shape) were not very practical; even at the time, they were criticised. In the 1850s, American Amelia Bloomer pioneered a startling new fashion: loose, baggy trousers under full, knee length skirts. Her invention – nicknamed 'bloomers' – never became widely popular. But, in the 1890s, female trousers were introduced again, as women began to take part in active sports.

Woman wearing 'bloomers', 1894.

Just for decoration

Between 1875 and 1900, fashionable women dressed in amazingly complicated styles. All were designed for good looks, not for comfort. Most were impossible to work in; they were symbols of wealth and luxury. Some had trains (trailing fabric at the back), or yards of elaborate drapery. In the 1880s, tight, straight 'tie-back' skirts made walking difficult, and shawl-like 'dolman' sleeves made it hard to move the arms. Hems, collars, cuffs, seams and lapels were all trimmed with frills, braid or embroidery. New men's fashions – apart from stiff shirt collars - were much more comfortable. They included relaxed jackets for evening wear (called tuxedos in the USA) and roomy knickerbockers (knee-breeches) plus tweed jackets for the country.

The dress of the bustle period swathed the lower half of a woman's body in numerous ruffles and pleats, often in light colours using vibrant new dyes.

Did you know...?
A fashionable female shape from around 1860 was known as a 'Grecian bend'.

WESTERN WORLD 1750-1900

The years 1750-1900 saw great technical and economic changes in Europe and the USA. New social groups developed: the working class and the middle class. Their lifestyles were reflected in their footwear.

Boots for heroes

This 19th-century cartoon shows the design of the first Wellington boots.

In 1776, the United States of America declared independence from Britain. To help fight back, the British hired troops from the Hesse region of Germany. These 'Hessian' soldiers wore distinctive knee-high leather boots. In the USA, they developed into the heeled boots worn by cowboys. In Britain, they became the basis of tough, riding boots, first worn by army commander the Duke of Wellington.

Spatterdashes

Fine shoes were expensive, and very delicate. So, since the 1600s, men and women had covered their shoes and stockings up to the knee with thick, strong leggings called 'spatterdashes' or 'gaiters'. But by the 19th century, gaiters fell out of fashion. They were replaced by a short, ankle-length 'spat' that filled the gap between the top of a shoe and the bottom of a trouser leg, or edge of a skirt hem.

Home Sweet Home

Middle-class families, who made their money from running businesses or working in the professions, placed great value on maintaining a spacious, comfortable, tranquil home. After returning home from work, men liked to relax in easy slippers or house shoes. These were made from soft fine leather, felted (boiled, compressed) wool, tapestry, or velvet.

A pair of 19th-century gentleman's slippers, embroidered with gold stitching.

Sweet and simple

For most of the 19th century, shoes worn by fashionable women were light and delicate. Out of doors, they wore high-heeled ankle boots made of kid (baby goat) leather, that fastened at the side with rows of tiny buttons. Indoors, they wore low-heeled slippers made of silk or fine leather. This delicate fashionable footwear was a great contrast to the sturdy wooden clogs and hobnailed leather front-laced boots worn by working-class women.

This 19th-century woman's silk slipper (right) was fastened by ribbons tied around the ankle.

Spats were made of stiffened fabric, in white (left), tan or grey. They buttoned neatly on one side, and were often held in place by a buckled strap that passed under the instep.

After 1750, machines replaced hand-workers in many industries. Fine jewellery was still created, slowly and carefully, by expert craft-workers. But new, cheap mass-produced jewellery was made on machines. Make-up and body-care products were also produced in factories.

A mourning locket, made around 1800. It shows a woman crying beside a burial urn (container for ashes), plus weeping willow leaves, a traditional symbol of grief.

Plain and dull

New kinds of jewellery appeared, as ideas about family, society and politics all changed. Mourning jewellery was especially popular in Britain, picking up the sentimental feeling of the Victoria era. It was made of sombre materials, such as dark ebony (a precious wood), or black jet, and often featured the name or portrait of the deceased and sometimes a lock of their hair.

Royal display

Kings, queens and nobles continued to wear large amounts of fabulous jewellery. Expert jewellery makers, like the Fabergé family of St Petersburg, Russia, specialised in 'luxurious objects' for royalty throughout Europe. These included pretty but useless items, such as jewelled Easter eggs.

Fabergé egg and necklace, circa 1900.

Did you know...?
The Cullinan Diamond is the largest diamond ever discovered on Earth. It was dug up in the new mines of South Africa in 1905, it weighed almost half a kilo.

Gold and diamonds

The USA had no royalty, but the Tiffany family of New York designed new ways of setting high-quality precious stones for rich business families to wear. Their products included 'solitaires' – large stones chosen for their brilliance, set alone on a ring. Gold for jewellery now came from California, where it was discovered in 1848, and from new mines in Australia and Africa. Rich deposits of diamonds were also found in South Africa during the 1870s. As a result, gold and diamond jewellery became very fashionable.

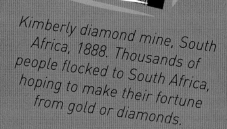

Kimberly diamond mine, South Africa, 1888. Thousands of people flocked to South Africa, hoping to make their fortune from gold or diamonds.

For celebrities

Fashionable jewellery-making companies also supplied diamonds to glamorous celebrities, such as actresses and opera stars. These women were famous and talented, but shunned by leaders of 'polite' society, who disapproved of their clothes, their make-up and their behaviour. Throughout the 19th century, respectable men and women stopped using perfume or cosmetics, except for faint flower scents and invisible skin cream. Coloured lips and cheeks, dyed hair, strong scents and powdered faces were said to be signs of immorality.

This painting Cinderella and Her Wicked Sisters *by Emile Meyer illustrates the Victorian attitude to excessive use of make-up which was frowned upon.*

WESTERN WORLD 1900-1950

In the early 20th century, new technology, continued to increase the range of cheap, mass-produced everyday clothes for ordinary people to wear. Clothing styles still followed high fashion, but were also influenced by social changes, economic crises, and two World Wars.

Regional variations

This group of poor people are washing clothes at an Italian street fountain.

In poor regions such as southern Europe, women wore dresses with aprons and shawls over the top. Men wore long, straight trousers, with shirts and jackets or waistcoats. Around the coast, fishermen and sailors preferred hand-knitted woollen sweaters. In the American West, farmhands and cowboys dressed in shirts and narrow jeans trousers made of tough blue denim. The design had been patented by Levi Strauss in the 1870s.

Wartime clothes

During World War I (1914-1918), millions of men were in uniform. Off duty, they wore clothes similar to late 19th-century peacetime styles. These included three-piece suits, worn by clerks in offices, and woollen jackets with thick trousers, for country workers. However, women's clothes changed dramatically, as they took over fighting men's jobs - driving trains, fighting fires and making weapons. For ease of movement, and for safety, they took off their stiff, wasp-waisted corsets and cut their skirts slightly shorter.

A stylishly dressed woman of the 'Flapper' era (1920s), modelling a loose fitting sleeveless dress and feather boa.

Work and leisure

In the 1920s and 1930s, male labourers working in factories, at construction sites, and on farms, wore all-in-one heavy cotton overalls. Men employed in shops and offices dressed in neat suits and ties. But for leisure wear, most men chose similar styles: relaxed, baggy trousers and a loose jacket or knitted sweater. Zip fasteners, mass–produced from the 1930s, replaced buttons and buckles for leisure wear.

America labourers pictured in the 1920s in casual clothing.

Uniform styles

Women's dresses in the 1930s became slightly longer, and more fitted, as a reaction to the 1920s boyish styles. In 1939, World War II began. Large numbers of women volunteered to join the armed forces, and, even off duty, their everyday clothes were based on sensible, masculine, uniform styles. Skirts were the shortest yet (knee length), with crisp pleats. Frocks had collars while jackets were short and square-shouldered, like men's.

A wartime costume (jacket and skirt) and dress, 1940. Legs were often bare, since silk and fine cotton, used for knitted stockings, were in very short supply.

71

WESTERN WORLD 1900-1950

At the start of the 20th century, fashions for the rich were similar to those of the late 19th century. But wars, social problems, and new ideas about politics, science and art all had an impact on fashion. In less than 20 years, the clothes people wore changed dramatically.

Bright Young Things

Millions of people died during World War I (1914-1918). As well as mourning the dead, those who survived were determined to change society, and to enjoy themselves. They went on protest marches, admired new, abstract art, and danced to shocking new music – jazz. Women cut their hair, threw away their corsets, and wore short, simple skirts that ended just below the knee. The fashionable 1920s female figure was young, fit and boyish.

Formal and frilly

Until around 1910, men's fashions were sombre, and women's very elaborate. For day, smart men wore black frock coats (a dress coat or suit coat) and grey trousers, or lounge suits (a business suit with matching jacket and skirt or trousers) with matching waistcoats. For evenings, they wore black trousers with tail coats or tuxedos. Women wore long dresses with bloused bodices, full skirts and tiny waists. Necklines were high for daytime, but low for evening wear. Corsets stiffened with whalebone were needed to achieve a fashionable figure.

Jewish community, 1905. The women are wearing long, decorated dresses.

Elegance returns

In the 1920s and 1930s, lounge suits, tweed sports jackets and grey wool trousers became usual daywear for men. Trousers now had turn-ups, and the legs were much wider. The most fashionable, known as 'Oxford Bags', measured 50 cm at the hem. Long, baggy breeches, called 'Plus Fours' were also popular. They were worn with sleeveless, hand-knitted pullovers in 'Fair-Isle' designs, which were knitted bands of patterns such as crosses, diamonds and stars. Fashions for women were elegant and ladylike.

By 1930, dinner jackets/tuxedos were fashionable for dances and parties. Women's evening clothes were long again.

Did you know...?

- The name for the style of suit known as 'the Tuxedo' came from Tuxedo Park, a district In New York State, where fashionable people lived.

The cloche hat

After the war ended in 1918, women refused to return to their earlier way of life - or style of clothing. They cut their hair and experimented with the world's first 'perms' (permanent waves). They wore tight-fitting 'cloche' (bell-shaped) hats with tiny brims, pulled low down over the face.

Cloche hats of the 1920s were plain, simple and easy to wear. They would only fit over short hairstyles.

WESTERN WORLD 1900·1950

The early 20th century was a troubled time. Millions of young men died in two World Wars (1914-1918 and 1939-1945); millions more families faced poverty, hunger and homelessness during the economic crises of the 1920s and 1930s. Many people felt lucky to have any shoes to wear; but footwear fashions changed fast for the fortunate.

At work and in wartime, ordinary men and women wore machine-made low-heeled, thick-soled, lace-up leather boots. Soldiers' boots were similar, but heavier and with hobnailed soles. Many people could not afford more than one pair of boots or shoes, so they looked after them carefully.

Functional footwear

Short·skirt styles

Women's lives changed fast in the early 20th century. They won the vote, trained for careers, and took over men's work in wartime. They cut their hair and wore short skirts; for the first time for thousands of years, their legs were on display. Fashion shoes were designed to flatter. Popular styles had medium heels and tapering toes, and were held in place by a bar across the instep.

Short skirts and American-designed 't-bar' shoes were ideal for dancing.

74

Neat feet

Smart footwear was an essential part of the stylish, tailored look favoured by fashionable young men with money. In town, they wore polished 'Oxfords' (neat lace-up shoes). In the country, they wore boots or 'brogues' (heavy laced shoes decorated with fancy stitching, punched hole patterns and tassels). In the USA, 'loafers' (slip-on shoes) and 'co-respondent' shoes (made with different coloured leathers) were fashionable.

These two-coloured 'co-respondent' shoes for men, made around 1930, are decorated with punched holes and zig-zag edging.

Sports and leisure

At the start of the 20th century, men and women wore laced leather boots for outdoor sports such as football and cycling. For sports played indoors or in summer, such as basketball and tennis, they wore lighter shoes with canvas uppers and flexible, cushioned, rubber soles. In the USA, manufacturers created a whole new kind of footwear based on sportswear designs. These 'sneakers' were comfortable and easy to wear, and became very popular with young people.

The 'Keds' brand of sneakers was launched in the USA in 1916. By the 1930s, as this shop window shows, there were many different styles.

WESTERN WORLD 1900-1950

The early 20th century was a time of rapid change in the arts. Old-fashioned rules of respectability and 'good taste' were cast aside. Some jewellery also used new, non-precious materials, made in factories.

Art Nouveau

A big design revolution that effected the style of jewellery became known as 'Art Nouveau' (French for 'new art'). Art Nouveau styles began in the late 19th century, and fell out favour around 1918. Designs often had a dreamy quality that reflected new ideas put forward by writers, scientists and philosophers. They included images of exotic plants and animals seen as unsuitable for jewellery before.

Art Nouveau sterling watch fob, featuring Art Nouveau-style women.

Art Deco

Another design revolution took place during the 1920s and 1930s. Called 'Art Deco' (short for Decorative Art), it was made famous by a huge international exhibition held in Paris, France, in 1925. Art Deco styles were sleek and streamlined, with smooth shapes, geometric patterns and neat, crisp details. Jewellers used industrial materials, such as polished steel, as well as silver and gold. They set small precious stones side by side to create 'pavé' (flat) bands of glitter or colour, instead of using larger, individual stones.

A dramatic 1920s costume enameled brooch featuring a peacock with an elaborate jewelled tail.

Hollywood style

By the 1930s, movies were the most popular mass entertainment in the Western world. Fashionable film-stars wore Art Deco jewellery and dramatic make-up, on and off screen. In France, companies such as L'Oréal (founded in 1909) pioneered new, scientific ways of manufacturing cosmetics. In the USA, in the 1930s, Max Factor created special make-up for film photography and won a prestigious Oscar award. Cosmetics were widely advertised in popular new women's magazines, and once again became respectable.

Actress Ginger Rogers in 1933, applying make-up in her Hollywood dressing room.

Real plastic, fake jewels

Did you know...?
In the early 20th century scientists discovered they could create rubies by flowing chemicals through a flame heated to around 2,000 °C.

The first plastic that could easily be moulded was invented in 1909 (by Leo Baekeland, a Belgian-born chemist living in the USA). It was widely used for jewellery and for other decorative items, such as buckles and buttons. Plastic could be cast (poured into moulds) to mass-produce fancy shapes that would take hours or days to carve by hand. It could also be coloured to imitate coral, turquoise, tortoiseshell and many other natural materials. Around the same time scientists experimented with ways of creating precious stones. In 1900, French chemist August Verneuil invented a way of making rubies that is still used today.

Colourful plastic buttons, made around 1910 in a wide variety of shapes.

WESTERN WORLD 1950-2000

In the second half of the 20th century, all kinds of clothing, from everyday garments to high-fashion designs, changed more quickly than ever before. Ideas about wearing clothes changed as well. There were fewer rules about 'correct' or 'suitable' dressing.

Utility

Many countries in Europe were devastated by World War II. Clothing was scarce, and hard to buy, and many governments rationed fibres and fabrics even after the war and added high taxes to luxury imports. They also encouraged citizens to not throw old, worn clothes away. Men's suits and women's dresses were plain and simple, used no unnecessary fabric, and were often patched or darned.

Utility styles for all the family in the early 1950s.

Marlon Brando in A Streetcar Named Desire in jeans and T-shirt.

Made in the USA

In the 1940s and 1950s, the USA was the world leader in popular entertainment. Blue jeans, seen in cowboy movies, began to be sold beyond Western states in the 1950s. American knitted cotton sportswear, such as polo-necks and T-shirts, replaced shirts made of broadcloth (woven fabric) for informal, everyday occasions. Comfortable but form-fitting cotton briefs were favourite male and female underwear. By the 1960s, new, artificial fibres, such as nylon (invented by US scientist Wallace Carothers) were used for everyday clothes.

Did you know...?
Before the 1960s, most Western women wore stockings and suspenders, but after the mini-skirt became popular so did tights.

Anything goes

The 1960s were a time of social experiment and political discontent. Young people rebelled against authority, and chose their own everyday clothes. These combined shapes, fabrics and decorations from many ethnic traditions with the latest high-fashion designs. For the first time, trends in everyday clothing were set by ordinary men and women, not by a rich, privileged elite. Although it provoked protests, women also began to wear trousers as ordinary, everyday clothes.

Sports-style clothes were first worn by young people, but were soon chosen by older men and women as well.

The most famous 1960s garment was the mini-skirt, which came up to 6 inches above the knee, pioneered by 'alternative' British designer, Mary Quant.

Sports wear spin-off

Everyday wear based on comfortable sports clothes was first made by French designer Coco Chanel in the 1920s and 1930s. By the end of the 20th century, mass-produced versions of sports-style clothes, such as shell-suits (a type of tracksuit), joggers and sweatshirts, were the Western world's most popular everyday leisure wear. New elastic fibres, such as Lycra (TM), invented in the USA in 1959, were added to knitted or woven fabrics during manufacture. They allowed a much closer fit, fewer wrinkles and gave extra flexibility.

WESTERN WORLD 1950·2000

After years of death and destruction caused by the Second World War, 1950s fashions for the wealthy and for everyday people became closer than ever before. New styles, designed by and made for young people, led to a revolution.

The New Look

In 1947, French designer Christian Dior introduced his latest Haute Couture collection. It caused a sensation! Soon nicknamed the 'New Look', it featured full skirts, tight waists, low necklines, high heels and feminine, curving outlines. 'The New Look' was a dramatic contrast to wartime uniform styles, and remained popular for years. It was not practical for everyday working wear, and could only be afforded by wealthy, leisured people.

Mini, Midi, Maxi

In 1965, young designers Mary Quant, from Britain, and Andre Courreges, from France, made the world's first mini-skirts. Styled as part of simple, shapeless 'shift' dresses, mini hemlines varied in length, but were all above the knee. Mini-skirts became immensely fashionable. They were worn with fashionable shoes or boots, and nylon tights - another 1960s invention.

By 1970, new calf-length (midi) and floor-length (maxi) skirts became fashionable for a while.

Paris fashions, 1952. Full 'New Look' skirts needed layers of petticoats underneath.

Thin, delicate 'Twiggy' (real name Lesley Hornby), photographed 1965.

Baby boomers

The 1950s saw the arrival of the influence of the baby boomer generation (people born between 1946–1964). They rebelled against the bland fashion of their parents. In the 1950s, male Greasers wore leather jackets and jeans to copy film stars such as Marlon Brando, while girls wore tight shirts, slim skirts and stiletto heels. Male Beats wore black sweaters and chinos while girls wore straight skirts, black leotards and sandals or ballet slippers. In the 1960s and 1970s, dazzling pyschedelic (colourful) styles were popular, as were hippy kaftans (full-length garments with long sleeves). In the 1970s and 1980s, Punk fashions with studs and zips became popular, as did Goth styles - black clothing with downbeat decorations.

A punk wearing a leather jacket covered in studs and zips.

Power dressing and 1990s fashion

In the 1980s, new political ideas inspired a new style known as 'Power Dressing'. Men and women 'yuppies' (Young Upwardly Mobile Professional Person) aimed for high-flying careers, and hoped to make lots of money. Free time was spent frittering away large sums of money. Men wore dark tailored suits, expensive shoes, shirts and ties, and trousers held up by red braces. Women wore straight, knee-length skirts and jackets with wide padded shoulders. In the 1990s, young people adopted a more urban look. Loose trousers and sportswear were popular, as were expensive designer clothes, including jeans by firms such as Calvin Klein and Guess, costing hundreds of pounds.

A fashion model wears a shirt with shoulder pads and white trousers during a 1980 fashion show.

Until the late 20th century, high fashion footwear was only worn by rich, privileged people. But mass media rapidly spread information about changing styles. And mass production methods made fashion footwear cheaper and more widely available than ever before.

High fashion

New footwear materials, such as metal and moulded plastic, made it possible for manufacturers to mass produce women's shoes with extremely thin, high heels. These caused an outrage when they first appeared in the 1960s. High heels can cause health problems such as shortened tendons and back problems, but despite this they remain popular. This pair dates from the 1990s.

High heels caused an outrage when they first appeared. Wearers were banned from many buildings as people feared that their spiky heels would damage the floor.

Designer fashions

Top shoemakers were often inspired by science – such as the flat, square-toed leather 'Space Age' boots (made for wearing with mini-skirts) of the late 1960s. Top shoemakers charged very high prices for custom-made creations, but cheaper footwear, based on their ideas, could be purchased by almost anyone.

The 1960s model Twiggy wearing pale lipstick and spiky false eyelashes.

Glitter, gloss and blusher

By the 1960s, a much younger look was preferred. This featured huge, child-like eyes with long, spiky lashes, a ghostly-pale complexion, and white or pale pink lipstick. New ingredients made fresh effects possible. Flakes of minerals, such as mica, created glittery, frosted eye-shadow; lip-gloss and blusher gave faces sheer, shiny colour. Jewellery in the 1960s was influenced by traditional Indian and African designs, and was often imported.

Did you know...?

Tattoos and body-piercing can be dangerous unless completely sterile (or disposable) equipment is used.

An couple pictured in the 1990s wearing rings and facial piercings.

Piercing, paint and chains

For most of the 20th century, toiletries for men were limited to soap, hair-cream and (sometimes) after-shave lotion. But by the 1970s and 1980s, young men were experimenting with products such as cleanser and hair-spray. 'Glam Rock' musicians made eye make-up popular; other young men aimed for a bronzed, surfer look. Rival music and fashion trends, such as Heavy Metal and Punk, featured face-paint together with body-piercing, tattooing, and massive metal rings and chains.

GLOBAL STYLES TODAY

Fashion is always changing. Every year fashionable shapes, styles, designs and decorations hit the market. But they all serve the same purpose. They offer people the possibility to identify themselves through what they wear.

Couture continues

Socialite Paris Hilton takes prime position in the front row of a fashion show.

New fashions are constantly created by trend-setting designers as they have been for hundreds of years. Their lines of Haute Couture originals are very expensive and can only be afforded by the very rich. But modern manufacturing techniques mean that millions of copies can be made and sold all round the world. The designers also put their names to Prêt-à-Porter (ready to wear) clothes, which make the most money. News of the latest Haute Couture styles can now be sent round the world in seconds using mobile phones and the Internet.

Fashion shows

Since the 19th century top designers have shown off their latest styles at fashion shows. A designer will create a collection of their designs, or line, for each season. Important people from the fashion world and the fashion press all attend, so a successful show can make or break a new designer's career. It is thought fashion shows, or "fashion parades" as they were then called, began in Paris in the 1800s. America started its own fashion shows in department stores, in the early 1900s.

Lily Cole on the catwalk.

The growth of the fashion world

Traditionally the capitals of fashion have been Paris, London, Milan and New York. However, this is beginning to change. Western countries have struggled economically from 2008 and shoppers have had less money to spend on fashion. However, the economies of Brazil, Russia, China and India are becoming stronger and the fashion markets there are doing big business. It is predicted the new capitals of fashion will one day be Mumbai (India), Moscow (Russia), Beijing (China) and Rio de Janeiro (Brazil).

Size zero

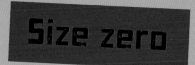

In recent years there has been a backlash against size zero fashion models, who are widely considered to be dangerously thin. Size zero (a size four in the UK) refers to the smallest size sold in American stores. In the early 2000s, it became increasingly fashionable to feature size zero models on catwalks and magazine covers. But several size zero models have died from malnutrition. In 2006, Spain and Italy banned size zero models from fashion shows. Parts of Brazil, Australia, India and Africa have also banned super thin models from being used.

Did you know...?
The first New York Fashion Week was held in 1943 to highlight the work of US designers.

Brazilian model Giselle Bündchen on the catwalk in Rio – an up-and-coming fashion capital.

GLOBAL STYLES TODAY

High Street shops are clever at copying recent fashion show designs and selling them at much cheaper prices. This happens very quickly and copies of catwalk designs can be in the shops within weeks of being shown. The Internet and mobile phones have all contributed to this speed.

Fashion fights back

High street shops have to be careful not to copy designs from luxury fashion houses too closely. Over the last decade many high street shops have ended up in court charged with plagiarising a designer's ideas. Trendy shoe designer Jimmy Choo successfully sued high street shop Oasis for copyright theft. The court agreed a pair of Oasis's £50 metallic wedge shoes were identical to a £355 Jimmy Choo design.

High Street designers

Fashion designers have become used to seeing cheaper versions of their Haute Couture originals in high street stores weeks after they were shown. So instead of fighting these shops, they have joined them. Many designers now create fashion lines directly for the High Street shops. Designer Zandra Rhodes offers a Topshop range, and Julien McDonald's first jewellery line has been launched at the budget jewellery retailer H. Samuel.

Zandra Rhodes has recently brought her quirky designs to the high street.

Celebrity fashion

High profile stars have always modeled a designer's clothes at important gala events, such as award ceremonies. The outfit is normally created especially for the star and the event, and raises the profile of the star and designer. But recently stars have been releasing their own lines of fashion in high street shops. Model Kate Moss launched a line of clothing at Topshop and Madonna has her own collection at H&M.

Kate Moss models at the launch of her own Topshop range.

Maintaining tradition

In many parts of the world, High Street fashion is of no relevance. Instead, people continue to wear traditional clothes. This is the case in many Muslim countries, where religious beliefs encourage all men and women to be modestly and traditionally dressed. Alternatively, some Muslims may choose Western clothes for home, but cover them with a traditional robe when they go out of doors. In many parts of India, Africa and South America, traditional styles are still favoured, especially for important occasions. People there feel proud of their clothing styles.

This Quechua woman is shown wearing traditional everyday clothing.

GLOBAL STYLES TODAY

In the early 2000s, the cost of Haute Couture fashion rose steeply, but the simple clothes sold in some High Street shops and supermarkets became cheaper and cheaper. This raised many fears about where the clothes were being made and the effect of cheap clothing on the environment.

Vintage clothes

In the early 21st century it became very trendy to buy vintage, or second-hand, clothing. Stars such as actress Lindsay Lohan spotlighted recycled fashion as a way of getting shoppers to trade in their unwanted clothing and cut down on their fashion purchases. Many US websites offered vintage clothes swaps. The website users swapped items of clothing over the Internet, not paying any money for the garments except for postage. In 2008, ex-model Twiggy started a UK TV show where women swapped their second-hand clothes.

Charity shops are the perfect place to recycle your clothes.

Disposable clothes

In recent years, companies and campaigners have worked together to end 'sweatshop' manufacturing such as this factory in Mumbai.

Over the last decade, many UK High Street shops and supermarkets offered cheap clothes at very low prices. The clothes were so cheap that it was feared customers had adopted a 'disposable clothes culture', throwing away the clothes they bought after wearing them only a few times. It was reported that many of these clothes were created in 'sweatshops'. Sweatshops refer to clothing factories in developing countries where workers have to work in terrible conditions for very little money. It is often said that sweatshop workers would never be able to afford the clothes that they make.

Cotton farmed organically is better for the environment.

Eco-fashion

Eco-fashion became very popular in the mid 2000s. Eco-fashion is all about environmentally friendly clothes that come from Fair Trade (see below).

Eco-friendly clothes are typically made from cotton grown without pesticides and with silk made by worms fed on organic trees. The clothes are not bleached or coloured using harmful chemicals. Sometimes the garments are made from second-hand clothes and even recycled plastic bottles. In the UK, High Street chains such as John Lewis and Marks & Spencer feature eco-friendly fashion ranges.

Fair Trade

Producers of clothing, cotton, silk and other materials in developing countries usually only receive a tiny amount of money for their produce. This is despite the fact that their produce is sold for many times more than the producer is paid. Fair Trade is a movement, which aims to help these disadvantaged people by offering them 'fair' terms of trade. There are several Fair Trade shops on UK High Streets, for example People Tree.

GLOBAL STYLES TODAY

Shoes have always been a big part of the fashion world, ever since high heels became trendy in Europe in the 16th century. While most modern decades have seen styles come and go, the 2000s were a mix of everything that came before.

Every shoe

In the 2000s, many styles returned that many shoppers thought were dead and buried. Cowboy boots, flip-flops, Wellington boots (otherwise known as 'wellies'), canvas sneakers, ballerina pumps and sandals all did big business on the high street. Many were also surprised to see the return of high heels; ranging from stilettos to wedge heels. Wedge heels are so called because they sit on a solid 'wedge' of cork, wood or leather. Designers such as Marc Jacobs, Hugo Boss and Gucci all released lines of Wedge shoes in 2008.

The Sex and the City effect

Using designer fashions on TV can make the designers nearly as famous as the stars of the show. This is true of the US TV series, Sex and the City. The star of the series, Carrie Bradshaw (played by Sarah Jessica Parker), was a shoe fanatic and made Manolo Blahnik shoes a household name. Other shoe designers to receive exposure from Sex and the City were Christian Louboutin and Jimmy Choo. These designer shoes cost hundreds – sometimes thousands – of pounds to buy.

Carrie Bradshaw with her latest Manolo purchase.

The genuine article: Gucci handbags.

Handbags

Handbags and shoes are the ultimate fashion accessories to compliment a new dress or outfit. Handbags first appeared in 14th-century Europe, although a type of bumbag made of animal skin can be seen in Ancient Egyptian hieroglyphics. From the 1940s, handbags became a leading fashion accessory. In the 2000s, the leading fashion houses such as Chanel, Louis Vuitton, Hermès and Gucci all created handbags costing thousands of pounds. Because they are so expensive, cheap imitations of these designer handbags can be found all over the world.

Trainers

Sports shoes, together with sneakers, have also inspired today's most popular footwear: mass-produced, brand-name trainers. These are worn by adults and children, for street wear and all sorts of activities. Trainers are mostly made of synthetic materials with cushioned soles and elaborate fastenings. The styles and designs of trainers are constantly changing. The 2000s saw the popular return of the Converse All Star, a canvas basketball boot first created in 1917.

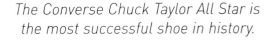

The Converse Chuck Taylor All Star is the most successful shoe in history.

GLOBAL STYLES TODAY

Make-up and jewellery has been used for thousands of years to enhance the wearer's looks, show off wealth, or advertise religious or superstitious beliefs. In modern times, the make-up market is worth billions of pounds and there are more jewellery styles than ever before.

Make-up

Catwalk make-up can be as dramatic as the clothes.

Beauty care is now a vast industry, controlled by multinational companies. They offer consumers countless new products in changing colours and textures. Some formulations are modern and high tech; others are based on traditional plant recipes. Organic make-up became very chic in the 2000s. Organic make-up is free from most chemicals and is not tested on animals. Make-up can look fashionable, flattering, messy, startling or cool.

Anti-aging

Anti-aging and beauty treatments drove the market in the early 2000s. Beauty products claimed to make the wearer look younger and the make-up promised to cover over anything that made the wearer look older. Plastic surgery also became more commonplace. Many clinics were set up to make surgery seem like a painless and quick procedure. Anti-aging procedures included laser treatments for skin conditions, face- and neck-lifts for sagging skin, liposuction to reduce layers of fat, and Botox injections to smooth out wrinkles.

In an age-conscious world, Botox injections have become increasingly popular.

Jewellery

Simple jewellery made from animal teeth and bones has been found dating back 40,000 years. Today's jewellery comes in a tremendous array of styles, materials and price ranges. Fake costume jewellery made a comeback in the mid 2000s, including cubic zirconia (a mineral that is used to imitate a diamond) or fake diamonds produced by man. Body piercing jewellery became commonplace in the 21st century. Studs, rings and jewels were fitted to ears, eyebrows, belly-buttons and even noses.

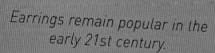

Earrings remain popular in the early 21st century.

Bling bling

In the early 2000s, glittering chains, rings, pendants and buckles became popular among hip-hop musicians and their male fans. They were made of real (or fake) diamonds set in heavy silver or gold; a few were even studded with flashing battery-powered LEDS. This lavish jewellery was known as 'bling'. It symbolised a love of money, a defiant attitude, youth, energy, power and pride.

Bling is a slang term to describe elaborate jewellery worn by hip-hop fans.

GLOSSARY

abayah Long, loose robe worn in Arab countries.

afterlife Continued existence after death.

amber Fossilised tree resin, used in jewellery.

amulets Lucky charms.

Anglo-Saxons People who migrated from North Germany to Britain around AD 500.

anorak Hooded, fur-lined tunic, worn by the Inuit people of the Eastern Arctic region.

barbarians Name given to peoples who did not speak their languages by the ancient Greeks and Romans.

batik A method of dyeing a fabric by which parts not intended to be dyed are covered with removable wax.

bodice Garment (or part of a garment) covering the upper part of the body, from the shoulders to the waist. Woman's laced outer garment.

bonnet Men: a baggy cap, with or without a brim. Women: a hood-shaped hat, often with a frilled or lace-trimmed brim, that fastens under the chin.

breeches Trousers that end above the knee.

brim The outer edge of a hat.

broadcloth Cloth woven on a loom.

brogues Thick, heavy shoes, designed for country wear. Often decorated with stitches, punched hole patterns and tassels.

buck skin Deer skin.

bustle Frame used to expand the fullness of the back of a woman's skirt.

calcaei Leather laced shoes worn by wealthy Romans.

caligae (plural) Boots worn by Roman soldiers. A single boot is called a 'caliga'.

cast Shaped by pouring hot metal into a mould.

chemise Long tunic, made of fine woven fabric, worn as an undergarment from the Middle Ages until the 19th century. A woman's loose, shirt-like undergarment.

clogs Thick, strong, backless shoes. Made entirely of wood, or with wooden soles and cloth or leather uppers.

cocoon Outer casing, usually made of spun thread, made by insect grubs to protect themselves while they are transforming into adults.

cosmetics Another name for make-up.

corset Medieval outer garment, worn to support and shape the waistline, hips, and breasts.

crinoline Hoop-shaped petticoat, stiffened with steel wire.

crown The part of a hat which covers the top of the head.

damask Rich patterned fabric of cotton, linen, silk, or wool.

democratic A place with majority rule.

dhoti Length of cloth, worn by Indian men. It could be wrapped round the body like a skirt or like baggy trousers.

diadem Decorative headband.

doublet Close-fitting tunic, worn in Europe in the late Middle Ages and 16th century.

drapery Clothing styled in loose folds.

drawers Long, loose underpants, worn originally by men and later also by women.

duck-bills Flat shoes with very wide toes, fashionable in the early 16th century.

ebony Dark, precious tropical wood.

emblems Symbols or badges.

enamel Thin layer of coloured glass fused (bonded by heating) on to metal.

engraved Cut into a flat surface.

Etruscans People who lived in Italy around 800 BC.

felt Thick cloth made of boiled, compressed wool or animal hair.

filigree Decoration made of fine, twisted wire.

Flappers Rebellious young women in 1920s Europe and the USA.

frock coat Man's coat with knee-length skirts.

gable A headdress worn by women in 16th-century Europe.

gaiters Waterproof fabric leg-coverings (also known as spatterdashes).

garland Circle of leaves or flowers.

gauze Fine, transparent fabric, often woven from silk threads.

gele Headwrap, worn by women in West Africa.

geta Wooden clogs worn by women in Japan.

granulation Jewellery decoration made from tiny balls of metal.

henna Reddish-brown dye made from crushed plant leaves.

heraldic Decorated with patterns or symbols showing membership of a noble family or loyalty to a lord.

Hessians High leather boots, with a notch at the top of the shin, originally worn by German troops fighting in the USA in the 1770s and 1780s.

hippy Young person who rebelled against social customs in the 1960s and 1970s, calling for love, peace and freedom.

hobnailed Studded with metal nails, to give extra strength and toughness.

hoop Dome shaped petticoat, strengthened with whale bone rods.

hose Stockings made of woven fabric.

instep The underside of the foot, between the toes and the ankle.

jade Smooth, hard green stone.

jet Hard, shiny black coal.

jubba Syrian name for a long loose robe, worn as an outer garment in many North African and West Asian countries.

kaftan Long, close-fitting robe, worn in Central Asia.

keffiyah Cloth-headdress worn in Arab countries of North Africa and the Middle East.

kente West African cloth woven in narrow strips then sewn together.

leather Animal skins that have been cleaned then treated (by drying, smoking or with chemicals) to preserve them.

leggings Leg-coverings made of woven cloth, knitted fabric or leather.

linen Clothes made from the flax plant.

loafers Flat, slip-on shoes with a flat piece of leather covering the instep.

lounge suit Suit consisting of a matching jacket and skirt or trousers.

moccasins Shoes made of a single piece of leather, gathered around the foot, worn by Native North Americans.

nemes Striped cloth headdress, worn in Ancient Egypt.

Oxfords Smart, flat lace-up shoes, typically with four sets of holes for laces.

Oxford Bags Loose fitting, baggy trousers popular in the early 20th century.

palm-fronds The long, thin leaves of date-palm and similar trees.

papyrus Reeds that grew in the River Nile.

parka Hooded, fur-lined tunic, worn by the Aleut people of the Western Arctic region. See anorak.

pattens Shoes with thick wooden soles, designed to keep the wearer's feet warm and dry. Sometimes called clogs.

peers Social equals.

peplos Long robe made of a length of cloth wound round the body and folded over with double layer of fabric for the bodice. Worn by women in Ancient Greece.

pillbox Small round, flat-topped hat without a brim. Named after the little cardboard boxes formerly used to contain pills.

pomegranate A fruit with a yellow-orange rind covering many bright-red seeds surrounded by juicy pulp.

poncho Cloak like a blanket with a narrow slit for a neckline, worn in South America.

prestige High status.

pschent Double crown, worn by pharaohs of Ancient Egypt.

psychedelic Mind-changing.

rosettes Circular decorations made of ribbon or braid.

sans-culottes Nickname for political revolutionaries in 18th-century France. They wore baggy trousers or kilts of rough linen; wealthy nobles wore culottes (knee-breeches).

sarong Length of wide cloth wrapped around the body. Worn in many parts of South-East Asia.

scarification Decorative pattern of scars made by cutting the skin.

shaman Magic healer.

silk A fine, lustrous material produced by certain insects to form cocoons.

slashed Cut with tiny slits to reveal an inner lining.

sole The lower part of a boot or shoe that touches the ground.

spatterdashes Waterproof fabric leg-coverings (also known as gaiters).

spats Short, smart gaiters. Often side-fastening, with buttons.

stola Outer tunic worn by women in Ancient Rome.

surcoat Over-dress (for women) over-tunic (for men). It was also worn over armour.

tailoring Cutting and sewing to fit the shape of the body.

tanned Coloured and preserved by soaking in chemicals.

tapestry Woven or embroidered picture or pattern.

tarboosh Cone shaped hat, traditionally worn in Turkey. Also known as a fez.

texture The appearance and feel.

toe-post A short, strong strap on a sandal that passes between the toes.

toga Semi-circular cloak, worn in Ancient Rome.

train Trailing fabric at the back of a skirt.

tribute Tax paid by conquered peoples.

Trunk-hose Short, thigh-length trousers, fastened at the bottom to create a pouched or puffed effect, worn in 16th-century Europe.

tunic Loose, usually sleeveless, garment which reaches to the thigh or knees.

turban A long strip of cloth wound round the head. Worn by men in Asia, and by male followers of the Sikh religion.

INDEX